WEATHERINGS

David Chorlton | Robert S. King
Co-editors

A Good Works Project

FUTURECYCLE PRESS
www.futurecycle.org

Library of Congress Control Number: 2015942324

Copyright © 2015 FutureCycle Press
All Rights Reserved

Published by FutureCycle Press
Lexington, Kentucky, USA

ISBN 978-1-938853-40-1

CONTENTS

Foreword..11

HOMELAND
Writings About Homelessness

Bint Arab..15
   Anagram (for the Ragman)...15
Shawn Aveningo..17
   They Call Me Mary..17
Mary Jo Balistreri..18
   Lady of the Rising Steam..18
Ruth Bavetta..20
   Los Angeles River..20
Nina Bennett...21
   For What It's Worth..21
Nancy Bevilaqua...22
   Transit (Lower East Side, 1989)...22
   Port Authority (Back Entrance), c. 1971..23
Alan Catlin..24
   From Bubbles to Bag Lady..24
David Chorlton..26
   A Day with no Address..26
   Eye to Eye...27
   First Night at the Shelter..28
   Vanished...30
Joan Colby...31
   Another Body Found in the Fox River...31
   Squatter's Rights..32
Steven Deutsch..33
   Flotilla..33
Julie Fowler..34
   Removing the Homeless from Church..34
M. Ayodele Heath...35
   On Closing Woodruff Park, Atlanta (for renovation for the 1996
      Summer Olympics)...35
Janis Butler Holm...37
   Why He Won't Eat the Hot Meal So Charitably Provided..............37
Paul Hostovsky...38
   Rewind..38

Laura M. Kaminski ... 39
   Red-Tailed Hawk ... 39
Robert S. King ... 40
   The Flashbacks of Lightning ... 40
Lidia Kosk ... 41
   The Clock's Ticking ... 41
Lee Kottner ... 42
   Discards ... 42
Carolyn Kreiter-Foronda ... 44
   Homeless on Independence Avenue ... 44
Cynthia Linville ... 45
   No Exit ... 45
Marjorie Maddox ... 46
   Between States ... 46
J. H. Martin ... 47
   Un Autre ... 47
Catherine McGuire ... 48
   Squatter's Flag ... 48
James B. Nicola ... 49
   The Sack Man and the Suitcase ... 49
Scott Owens ... 51
   Leonard ... 51
   Meadow: Mary and Joseph ... 52
Connie Post ... 54
   Extremities ... 54
   Your Doorstep ... 55
Sarah Russell ... 56
   Urban Sovereign ... 56
Paul Saluk ... 57
   End Game ... 57
J. J. Steinfeld ... 58
   Until the Paperwork Is Done ... 58
Wally Swist ... 60
   Amputee, Miami, 1959 ... 60
Sherre Vernon ... 61
   Why You Walk Alone ... 61
Lillo Way ... 62
   11th and Pine ... 62
Richard Widerkehr ... 64
   Homeless ... 64

METAMORPHOSIS
Writings About Aging

Peggy Aylsworth 67
   Giving Thanks 67
Nina Bennett 68
   Déjà Vu 68
Marion Brown 69
   Subway 69
David Chorlton 70
   Night Thoughts 70
Carl Chrisman 71
   Our Evenings 71
Beth Copeland 72
   Keeping Time 72
James Croteau 73
   Cover Boys 73
Anthony DiMatteo 74
   Assistive Learning 74
Heather Dobbins 75
   Lunch Hour in the Nursing Home 75
   P-H-E-N-O-M-E-N-O-N 76
Bonnie Durrance 77
   Mother is Coming 77
   My Mother in John Muir's Wood 78
Laura Foley 79
   Ode to My Feet 79
Taylor Graham 80
   Father, Son 80
Karen Greenbaum-Maya 81
   Dignitas 81
   Birdie 82
Nancy Gustafson 83
   On the Edge 83
   Aunt Saphrana Counsels 84
Lois Marie Harrod 85
   The Widow Laments Another Autumn 85
Karen Paul Holmes 86
   She Sat Alone in a Red Sequined Sweater on December 20 86
Paul Hostovsky 87
   Pearl in Bubble Wrap 87

Ann Howells..88
   Mom and Pop..88
A. J. Huffman..89
   Aging in an Instant..89
   My Body is Turning Against Me..........................90
   My Bladder is Shrinking...91
Joseph Hutchison..92
   First Bird at First Light..92
Robert S. King..93
   Mirror at the Speed of Light.................................93
   The Light Sedative of Dark....................................94
   Prescriptions for Two..95
   Strategy for Longevity...96
Judy Kronenfeld...97
   Her Vacated House...97
   At the YW Indoor Spa...98
Lori Lamothe...100
   Gray Sisters to Perseus..100
   Road Trip to Forever...101
   Red Barn in Snow...102
Linda Lowe...103
   Voices from Twilight Time Garden Villas........103
Stephanie Madan..106
   Albert Came, Too..106
John McKernan...107
   The Age Of Reason...107
James B. Nicola..108
   Another vase of flowers..108
Lynn Pedersen..109
   My Grandmother Peels Apples for Sauce........109
   How to Move Away..110
   At Forty..112
Richard King Perkins II..113
   The Impertinence of Ice..113
Jean Queneau...114
   Terminus...114
Mary Ricketson...115
   Walnut..115
   Stones at Sunset...116
   Alacrity..117
Kristin Roedell..118
   My Mother's Russian Caretaker.........................118

Suzanne Schon 119
    Just Leaves 119
Lucille Gang Shulklapper 120
    Aging 120
    Old Woman Plays Piano 121
Judith Skillman 122
    Trouble 122
    The Children Grow 124
Carol Steinhagen 125
    Dancing 125
    Body Art 126
Carole Stone 127
    Verona Park 127
Meryl Stratford 128
    Elegy with Backward Clocks 128
Laurence W. Thomas 129
    Aging 129
Sara Toruño-Conley 130
    Mother's Aftermath 130
Lillo Way 131
    Celestial Fantasy for Dr. Alzheimer 131
Abigail Wyatt 132
    Bluebells, An Elegy in Late Spring 132
    Everything She Said 133
    Kissing Is a Young Person's Game 134
James K. Zimmerman 136
    Old Letters From Myself 136

OUR PLACE
Writings About the Earth

Paula Ashley 139
    Sunset Vista 139
Ruth Bavetta 140
    Odette on the Sand 140
Marion Brown 141
    Lament in Many Chapters for the End of the Earth and Love 141
Jefferson Carter 143
    Nature Was My Church 143
David Chorlton 144
    In the Steps of the Rain 144
    Sky Island Encounters 146

Allison DeLauer 147
    The Muriana Poems 147
    Kaweah River Landscape 149
Bill Glose 151
    Kudzu 151
Lynn Hoffman 152
    River Song 152
    after the ocean left town 154
Karen Paul Holmes 155
    Flowers for You, Japan 155
Joseph Hutchison 156
    Auger 156
    The Gulf 157
Laura M. Kaminski 161
    Educating the Creek 161
Lee Kottner 162
    Advice for City People Who Move to the Country 162
Carolyn Kreiter-Foronda 164
    The Bay's Tributaries 164
Lori Lamothe 166
    American Primitive 166
    Museum of Natural History 167
    Cave of the Great Galleries 168
    White Pines 169
Laura LeHew 170
    Apis Mellifera 170
James B. Nicola 171
    Damsel Earth 171
Scott Owens 172
    Owned 172
Lee Patton 173
    Everlasting Trespass 173
    Field Study in Disturbed Soil 174
Lynn Pedersen 175
    How to Speak Nineteenth Century 175
    The Rift 176
Linwood Rumney 177
    Low Tide in Penobscot Bay 177
Eric Paul Shaffer 179
    Yadokari: Hermit Crab, Okinawa 179
Wally Swist 180
    In the Shade of a Cave 180

Lillo Way 182
    High Winds 182
    Death in Big Sur 183
    Foraging 184
Martin Willitts, Jr 185
    Communion with the Trees 185
Diana Woodcock 188
    Dugong 188
    Desert Ecology Lesson 19: Angiospermae—Dicotyledoneae 190
Ray Zimmerman 191
    Water 191

Contributors 193
Acknowledgments 209

FOREWORD

These writings have not been gathered under the illusion that literature can do anything to house those who sleep on the streets, turn around the trend towards a dramatically changing climate, or grant comfort and reassurance to the elderly. These themes have been chosen, however, in part because they rarely receive due attention in the political language of our time. There are elected representatives who would love to take away Social Security and think about how to do it between speeches that go against what the majority of scientists see as being beyond argument with regard to rising temperatures and what that implies for life on this planet for all species. To them, the homeless are an eyesore without a history. The most attention they receive is when a city is to host a major sporting event and concerns itself with sanitizing the streets so as not to be embarrassed when the visitors pour in.

As editors, we wanted to make the point that one can address problems with imagination and good writing. Poetry, especially, has become isolated from society as a whole and has a following primarily among other poets. This need not be the case, as we think that these pages contain work that can be appreciated by the public at large as much as by fellow writers. *Weatherings* may set an example both in establishing priorities and in using language to better observe and understand them. Being sensitive to the natural world is the first step toward preserving it. Applying the same standards of observation to the city, we encounter too many people carrying bedrolls or with nothing at all to carry, often talking loudly to nobody in particular, and with nowhere to cool off in the summer but the public library. As for old age, it may not be glamorous yet, but seeing Bob Dylan interviewed in the AARP magazine creates hope that our later decades will remain productive ones.

This is a book conceived as having a use beyond giving its contributors another line in their resumes. While its themes are familiar to everyone, the viewpoints here should open new ways to think about them.

—*The Editors*

HOMELAND

Writings About Homelessness

BINT ARAB

Anagram (for the Ragman)

Sam pushed the lid of the dumpster higher, and the stench of garbage clawed at him. The thing was so big, he could have laid a queen-sized mattress in it. He nearly fell in when he climbed the side and leaned over the edge to sift through the trash. People living in the condos along the alley usually left something good there on Friday nights, but not this time. Oil and bits of melted cheese stained the inside of a pizza box, but there weren't any crusts or slices of pepperoni left. The McDonald's bag held just an empty crushed burger wrapper. He pulled a newspaper out, checked the headlines, and then threw it on the ground by the bin. Something white caught his eye when he reared to leave; he grabbed a corner and pulled a flannel swatch out. Yellow trim and letter blocks decorated the blanket. No stains, just a little rip. It smelled like a baby.

Sam folded it and tucked it into his shopping cart. He put the newspaper on top of everything and wheeled the cart to the park, thinking about garbage bins and breakfast.

His morning route had disappointed him. Sam struggled to push his cart over the gravel path to get to a park bench. He needed to decide between going to "restaurant row" or the fast-food joints by the mall. Which bins would have more in them?

A boy about eight or nine years old walked toward Sam and scrambled onto the bench facing the backrest. "You a ragman? 'Cuz you sure got a lot o' rags."

Sam looked at the boy's ripped shirt and snorted. "Are you a runaway? 'Cuz you sure smell like one." Sam made a show of waving the air in front of his nose.

The kid giggled.

"Go home, boy."

"My name's Trevor."

"Whatever. Go back to your mama."

"Hain't got one."

"Everyone's got a mama."

Trevor stuck a finger in his nose, dug something out, and wiped it on his shirt.

Sam screwed his face up in disgust. "Aw, don't do that—wipe it on the grass!"

"So, you a ragman?"

"Where do you sleep?"

Trevor shrugged. Sam pulled the baby blanket out of his cart.

"Here—it's gonna be cold tonight. Sleep under a bench so no one can see you. Put the blanket on the ground beneath you, not on top of you. Hey! Are you listening?"

Trevor looked down at the pastel A-B-C's but didn't move to take the little blanket from Sam.

"Have you eaten anything for breakfast yet?" Sam asked.

The boy shook his head.

"Okay, come with me."

A wheel on the cart squealed and moaned as Sam pushed it over the grass to the park exit. He didn't turn to check that Trevor was following. He was thinking about how he'd been eight years old once too.

SHAWN AVENINGO

They Call Me Mary

I walk along 12th Street, meander aimlessly. It's Indian
Summer, and the scent of chicken noodle soup mixes with
the smell of a season's worth of humility. I search the parking
lot for a space, a place where I can keep one eye on my
shopping cart while I stand in line for a hot cup of coffee.
I continue to wander, wondering all the while what they see,
the strangers who examine their shoes as they pass by, preventing
any accidental meeting with my eyes. I keep hoping someone
will glance long enough to recognize me, to call out my name.
A woman calls me Mary, tilts her head in that confused
puppy dog way. The tilt of my head mirrors hers, as she
hands me a five dollar bill. I take the money, fold it meticulously
before placing it next to my tired heart. Tomorrow I can tell
them *My Name Is Mary.* I will watch the barista scribble it
with a black sharpie and draw a happy face on the white paper
cup. It will be a most delicious cup of Joe.

MARY JO BALISTRERI

Lady of the Rising Steam

Philadelphia, November 1976

Into the ice-edged darkness, my husband
and I hurried in the weak light of jaundiced
lanterns. Chestnut vendors huddled
into themselves, their fiery coals hissing.

Wind howled as we turned
the corner on Walnut Street, ripped off my hand-
loomed scarf and sent it flying.
I didn't know it was gone
until I heard the voice,
a wailing cry in the night.
A woman crouched over the grate,
my red silk
scarf thrashing
from a withered hand.
Unkempt, her face was pocked and ridged
with wrinkles. Garments of neglect hung
on the skeletal frame as she hovered in the warmth
of the manhole's rising steam. We stopped,
uncertain. She grabbed the hem of my coat.
Fear met the madness of her roving eye.

In the shelter of our car, she spoke to us
of art and architecture, insisted that her son was
a great industrial artist.
We talked close to an hour before we scrunched
bills into her hand, gave her our address
and drove away. She bent back into the black
starless night and we re-entered our comfortable life.

Months later, a police captain called
to tell us she was dead,
our name in her pocket,
the only clue to her life. A life we had forgotten.

Thirty years later, she is still the face I don't know,
and the face I'd know anywhere.
Sometimes on a foggy night,
or walking the cracked sidewalks of my small town,
I see the open hand so near, the bent body I want
to call back.

RUTH BAVETTA

Los Angeles River

Slow trickle of water,
buildings rigid on either side
like church elders in the sun.

A man comes up from the riverbed
where he sleeps under the bridge,
weeping, California winter
a habit around his shoulders.

He hesitates, pulls
from his rocky understanding, sentences.
I left the house, the family,
the life. I never knew
it would be so easy.

He folds his arms
against help or explanation,
his voice white as the concrete
of the riverbed. Easy, he says
and the wafer of truth rolls in his mouth
like the ooze of green water.

NINA BENNETT

For What It's Worth

Kicked out of a halfway house
for fighting after he threw away
his Haldol. Picked up on a parole
violation, he started an inmate riot,
spent time in solitary. His sister
wouldn't let him stay in her home.
The last time he lived with her
he called her toddler Satan,
said he had to be banished
from the kingdom.

He survived on the street
for a year, in a cardboard
container under the interstate.
Found a washing machine box,
carved doors between the two,
called it his condo. Guilt
consumed his sister as the virus
devoured him. She left a down
comforter on his doorstep.

In the ER he demanded leeches
to draw out his bad blood. Told the doc
the government gave him AIDS.
Threw a chair at a social worker,
earned another involuntary psych commitment.
Released after 72 hours, he walked 40 miles
to escape accusations screamed
by demons, crossed the state line.

That was 8 months ago. The clinic
called his sister, said he never
refilled his antivirals. She says
all she wants is for her brother
to die in a bed.

NANCY BEVILAQUA

Transit (Lower East Side, 1989)

Pigeons and the spikes to drive them off.
Sick men sleeping in the heart. (Tall one in a bag.
Bodega's always open, lit, someone looking on.
The fucking cough. Three more cigarettes
to hold you until dawn and 60 milligrams
of methadone.) Summer: skull of subway art,
spread yourself against the wall it's almost cool
beside the fan. Turnstiles heavy, unforgiving
(go under if you can I'll watch for you).

Craters of some stranger's eyes. Contagion
from the blood and lips of those you loved
(however long it breaks my skin I'll let you in).

Winter: buses run in snow between meridians
and guess how slowly they can go with someone
underneath. Cremation at the steps outside the church:
there's dust and hallelujah at the last door open
for the night. Purchase tickets at the gate
with whatever you've got left, if anything.

NANCY BEVILAQUA

Port Authority (Back Entrance), c. 1971

Tell me if the girl who held the pigeons underfoot was talking to her God or just felt left aside, the stairway hot with inner braking, huff of buses underground, fumes that would not carry to the suburbs. Maybe I was ten.

Mostly I had been caressed by drifts of normalcy, raised in white-child sacristy, and then she undisturbed my innocence (as if I knew a tired girl from a junkie). I thought she might be sick (she was). I wondered

why we didn't stop (no one does). 9th Avenue symphony. Her fingers wrecked beneath the shirt. She might have talked to me but see how tired we get of this; there's nothing left to give. (She's starving but she'll probably live.)

ALAN CATLIN

From Bubbles to Bag Lady

In the yearbook she was:
athletic, cheerful, class brain,
"smooches in the hallway,"
nickname, "Bubbles."
National Honor Society, Softball
Field Hockey, Band, Chorus,
Spanish Club, Latin Club,
Salutatorian. Played the classics
as privately taught prize pupil,
blue ribbon winner, on a Steinway
grand. Owned reams of bound
annotated scores: the Germans,
Austrians, Russians, pencil marked
in the margins with a shorthand of
her own devising. Was an amanuensis
to voices no one else could hear:
"Inscribe the secrets. No one else must
ever learn the truth."

Where did it all go wrong?
Not on Upstate liberal arts college
campus, earning a bachelor of arts in
business but somewhere else along
the ivy covered, post-commencement
path, to a cold, industrial complex campus,
that first voluntary commitment ten
years later, where she was shocked into
insensibility, rehabilitated and let go
until everything around her collapsed:
her marriage, her jobs, her life at home.
Everything gone as South as a subway could
carry her to the next involuntary commitment
twenty years later; aptly described in letters as,
"two years in hell with free drugs" and all
the spare time she needed to formulate bullshit

to confuse the doctors and to plot her revenge
upon all those people who put her here,
knowing full well, at some point, like in two years,
they had to let her go.

Which is how she ended up in the City,
one step removed from the street, unsupervised,
untreated, unaccountable for any new violent
crimes committed. Just another gaunt, denim
bag-toting old lady in second hand clothes,
hopping from one place to another, chain smoking
menthol shorts, Kool's with the filters broken
off, whispering to herself words, only she,
and the creatures inside, could understand.

Sometime she pauses in her travels from
place to place to listen, rapt, a smile on her face,
content knowing what only she, and the chosen
ones who travel with her, could ever hope to know.

DAVID CHORLTON

A Day with no Address

With a trace of Asia in his January face
an old man on Central Avenue
progresses two inches with each step
in athletic shoes that run on empty

to the corner where nomads talk
themselves warm beside shopping carts
loaded with old newspapers and rain.
As the sun goes down behind

the freeway on-ramp
the holder of a message written
in felt tip marker on cardboard
cut with a knife edge of cold

moves from car to car,
but misfortune is the only star
and the thermometer is stuck
at the freezing point of charity.

DAVID CHORLTON

Eye to Eye

Some faces don't look back
when looked at
but continue staring into
the space in front of them
at something only they can see.

It's easy to act
as if we don't notice
the crust across the skin,
the hair
growing into a tangle,
or the speed at which the complexions
have aged.

So we avoid having to decide
on a greeting appropriate
to the moment
when nothing comes to mind

to say to a person who looks
like a castoff
from a time of plenty
when plenty isn't enough

and while others live
can only survive.

DAVID CHORLTON

First Night at the Shelter

The line at the shelter just before seven
runs along a fence and back
around the corner of a building
whose beds are already filled. Patience
is the ticket, and waiting
becomes so easy as to make the time
pass gently. Some men are reading, others
talk in low voices about a bus ride
they took long ago that brought them
to this city in the sun, whose winters
are the kindest roof they can hope for,
each with his bag or a bundle
tied together with resignation. Women too
stand in shoes so heavy
it hurts to walk. The first bus stops,
fills up, and pulls away
for an unnamed destination
as the night chill drifts across the faces
of those remaining. This will be your first ride,
the night you never expected
to fall, when you go to sleep in the company
of strangers and share a meal
cooked over slow hunger. Your appointment
book is folded as small
as your insurance card, and tucked
into a pocket with a five dollar bill
and change that gets smaller
each time you count it, the way
news bulletins lose significance
once you have come this far. A few blocks away
a different world exists in the same city
as the one you now inhabit,
where the mail never comes and the clock
has a minute hand only. Your bus

arrives. It purrs to offer comfort
as you climb aboard, and you know
it is the best you can hope for
when your return address
is your memory.

DAVID CHORLTON

Vanished

We called her the Stroller, the lady
who swung one arm when she walked
and held the other to attention.
One day she washed her hair
in our lawn sprinkler. That was years ago,
too many to remember when
she walked the downtown streets
dressed in a raincoat as wrinkled as her face.
The pace of her steps suggested
she was going somewhere, had business there,
but we knew business would hold
its nose in her presence. We knew that for most
she was invisible, and only we
had a name to describe her. Once I greeted her
in passing because she was familiar
like a neighbor. It was just Hello
and a slight nod to acknowledge her.
But she kept her eyes
pointing down, scowled, pressed a shoe
hard into the pavement
and walked like a wind-up toy
with her swinging arm stiff. It hurt
to be ignored. Although we still noted
each sighting of her, reassured that she
was still as alright as a person can be
living as she did. Then a summer passed,
a year, and her absence reminded us
of her. On the hottest days she let her coat hang
open, but wore a woolen hat pulled tight
as her scalp. Until the day
she stopped outside our house, placed
her plastic sack of whatevers on the grass,
knelt in the spray of water, and shook
the dust out of her hair. It was grey mostly,
with dark brown streaks.

JOAN COLBY

Another Body Found in the Fox River

Sometimes, they roll
Off the lip of concrete
Into the river. Too drunk
To wake or thrash
When the current folds them
Into its dark cloak.

Sometimes, a struggle
Over territory. Each claims a spot
Along the bank or beneath
The bridge's span.

Grimy tents, scribble of rags,
A crippled shopping cart
Swiped from Safeway. What's
Left of a man distilled
In wine or whiskey.

Somebody shoved, somebody
Lost his grip. The river travels south
From dam to dam. Somebody
Fishing, hooked
A collar or a sleeve.
Somebody knows who it is.

JOAN COLBY

Squatter's Rights

Ensconced in a makeshift tent
On public property—like a bird's nest
Over the courthouse door—in this case
A library's arcade, he has grown
Into an icon sea-bearded as Poseidon
Ranting about how the waves of judicial decision
Have rendered him impotent—all this because
Of a $75 ticket for jaywalking
Years back when he used to venture forth
To community meetings to complain
About something or other. Passersby
Leave money which he says is only his due
Misused as he has been. A curiosity
Many view as a local celebration
Of a diversity they'd like to brag of
Their own bright tolerance like an antique gaslight
On the drives of their suburban homes
Not the embarrassing fiat of that woman
Ranting on the six o'clock news "I didn't
Move here to look at someone like that."

STEVEN DEUTSCH

Flotilla

You left behind
one half a jelly donut,
stale as last Wednesday;
some clothing, moth-eaten
and mildewed; two shoes,
one black, one brown,
with newsprint for the soles.
You left behind a paper sack
of winter warmth, and poetry
by Whitman, Poe and Crane,
well-fingered and browned in age.

You walked into the river
and left behind four dollars
and eighteen cents, which I
have spent on coffee
and a banana nut muffin
that crumbled in its freshness.

Your poetry, penned
in your perfect prep school hand,
was stuffed inside two newish socks
atop the brown and laceless shoe.
It is unnervingly good,
but I can use the socks.
I crumpled your words in their freshness,
and set them to sail upon the river,
page by remarkable page.

JULIE FOWLER

Removing the Homeless from Church

Under buttressed and vaulted gold-star deep blue
    I sit in this subdued house of grace
    and rest from the city's urgency.

Gold-haloed Mary shines in spotlight
    listening to petitions for blessing
    near the wink and glow of votives
    burning hopes skyward.

Few are here this weekday noontime
    as dark-carved apostles solemnly guard
    those who pray.

Hidden in shadows, a rumpled, sleeping man
    is roused from his pew by custodians
    and quietly ushered away from refuge,

While stone angels kneel over the founder's centograph
    and a blood-cleansed crucified Jesus
    stoically hangs from his cross.

M. AYODELE HEATH

On Closing Woodruff Park, Atlanta (for renovation for the 1996 Summer Olympics)

exhaling...
        icicle-clad, sky-blue breath
    inhaling...
               sharp, cold metallic abandon...

They've closed Woodruff Park where, last summer,
    Brother Johnson, in a striped bow-tie
        one of the brothers from The Nation gave him
        at the shelter back in '87 (he was so proud),
        preached his daily sermon to a crowd
        of no fewer than two hundred
        about *the power of Black Nationalism*
        & how Geronimo Pratt is still in prison
        & Mumia Abu Jamal still ain't free; and

Sister Mabel *Boydidyoucombyohairthismawnin?* Davis
    was always makin sho the city clean
    when all dem White folks n' Japs come in 1996.
    You don't want dem goin back n' tellin' dey people
    Atlanta's a nasty city wit trash all ovah da ground.
    I mean you wouldn't invite company 'round
    yo house if you hadn't cleaned up, wouldya? unaware
    of her pending eviction notice
    as she picked up a policeman's
    abandoned Dunkin' Donuts bag; and

Mister Haynes (he nothing to lose, I a friend to gain)
    bet me lunch he could checkmate me
    in ten moves (it only took seven)
    & I bought him a sandwich at Michael's Deli.
    Best meal I had since Hosea's dinnah last Christmas season.
    Turkey & Swiss. No pork. Brother Johnson say
    dat's blue-eyed devil food. With ridged corn chips.
    Man, I ain't had dese in...

        a luxury I guess
                when you are homeless—
                        when your home
                address is
        Woodruff Park.

        All that hair must be hot
                I thought. But
                        it must be warm
                        in the winter (in this air
                that hurts to breathe.)

I wonder
        if Black turns to blue
                        when you're that cold,
                        old, low & forgotten
by this progressive city of lofty,
                glass skyscrapers
                        full of stonethrowers
                        who've never walked a mile
even in their own shoes.

Holding the mayor's free
        one-way bus ticket
        to AnywhereButHere
                if you'll just sign this contract
                        that you'll never come back.

        Heartless January
                shrilling
                        like an angry woman
                You are nothing
        in your ear.

        I wonder
        where they live
        now

JANIS BUTLER HOLM

Why He Won't Eat the Hot Meal So Charitably Provided

He sees how the lettuce
slides around the plate,
yellow and cunning,
mysterious in its ways.

He notes that the fries
are pointing southeast,
that they are sharp and oiled
and spattered with red.

The tomato slices whisper
soft pink obscenities,
their harlot song calling
to his lips, his tongue.

He smells in his burger
the black, smokey flesh
of things small and tender.
And he's back at My Lai.

And he's up and running,
he's running, and around him,
the jungle, the colors,
the chaos, the horror.

He's running and stumbling
and heaving and moaning.
He's running, and he's thinking
that he wants to go home.

PAUL HOSTOVSKY

Rewind

The homeless are giving their money
to poor you and me, stalled here
in traffic, waiting to get home
to the lost and hopeless suburbs.

They're reaching into their little cups
and giving away whatever
their fingers happen to touch first,
and without thinking twice.

The clouds pass weirdly overhead
as you and I roll down our windows
and look directly into the faces
of our backing-away benefactors

whose eyes are rolling counterclockwise
as the balked and steaming traffic
backs up all the way into the obscure
streets of the impoverished heart.

LAURA M. KAMINSKI

Red-Tailed Hawk

On the way to the park at the edge
of the marsh where you can stop
and sleep in safety while the river
feeds the lake, there is a broken
billboard that used to mark the turn.
Its painted letters are now ghosts,
legible only when it's cloudy.

A red-tailed hawk is perched above
the faded smudge that used to be
an "A." His vision is precise—
he can even see the mice
as they creep beneath the fluttering
seed-heads of the grass across the road.

Readable or not, this is our sign—
we reach it and walk west
along the gravel track. I take a break
to turn and stretch and watch the hawk,
wonder about his landmarks, his kind
of map, how it is he knows

while he's up in the high-sky
soaring thermal heat and drifting,
which way is east, which way and when
he must return each night to watch
the sun's slow sinking
from right here.

ROBERT S. KING

The Flashbacks of Lightning

The beard who sucks his thumb
moves every day to a different
cardboard foxhole, never sleeps
in the Shelter, that orphanage
for grown-ups.

The few who've known him long
say his younger mouth was always
open, a hollow ring, a silent shout,
the calm before the storm.

Streetmates call him Stormy,
one who storms in, storms off,
who sleeps with a night light
of lightning and remembered rain.

Name-tags still chain his neck,
his rank sewn like a scar on the sleeve.
The only pocket without holes
keeps an old picture of a private
waving to cheers of confetti,
another of a hippie saluting
with a dirty finger, as if to be a man
is to choose which camouflage
to wear, duty deciding to believe
that the flag never hits the ground
nor ever drapes a coffin.

Rags of his jungle coat fly
in a wind never at home.
Sucking on the barrel of his thumb,
his stare seems to follow the distant
thunder, a wandering echo
seeking the voice that made it.

LIDIA KOSK

The Clock's Ticking

(translated by Danuta E. Kosk-Kosicka)

The green curtain
outside my window
lights

In grandeur
leaves fall
like gold dust

The window of tree's heart
unveils
hope of luscious grass
fades away

Birds' claws drape
trains of sorrow
November grows dim

The clock's ticking

From behind the dark cabinet
of life's clock
time rolls out to awaken
the outside world

It cuts off winter's path
unexpectedly
spring wafts on the wind

Before a man can look
through the window
his movements are stopped
on the face of his wrist watch

Trees bear new leaves
among broken glass
blades of wounded grass
climb up

The clock's ticking

LEE KOTTNER

Discards

They lie on the sidewalk in their boxes,
beauty hidden inside, peeping out,
though clearly abandoned.
We pass them by, only mildly curious.
One or two of us may stop,
carefully lift a lid, peer inside, rescue
one unwilted flare of color.
We are a little ashamed of ourselves,
not for coming away with such loveliness for free,
but to be seen picking through refuse
however unlike trash it is.
Here, on this side of town,
the preference is to buy new
or so old that the object
is beyond the taint of cast-off
or second hand.
So we leave the boxes and their contents
where they lie, no matter
what splendor lurks within.

We prefer to keep our hands clean.

But wait long enough
and one with less discrimination
and hands already Augean with other such foraging
will stop.
And he does. He too has lain in a box on the sidewalk
and there was a certain beauty
locked in there too. Like calls to like.

He flings open the found boxes
like a pirate with a treasure chest,
and so it is—sold, each bloom the means
to a hot meal, a room instead of a box.

Radiance spills out, leaves and wild harlequin petals
in all their mercy.
He reels back, staggered,
looks at his begrimed hands,
face writ with despair.
Shakes his head—

Walks away.

CAROLYN KREITER-FORONDA

Homeless on Independence Avenue

Who can say how long he will
lie here, spanning the grate
like an aging bridge clinging
to life? Six p.m., he claims
his territory, back turned
toward the Capitol dome,
toward Freedom flickering
in the weary sun. I look up
at a street light, the bulb
broken, slivers strewn
over the victim's coat.
The old man rises to his knees,
and in his lapel a tulip grows,
so bold it outlives the chill.
Steam from the grate enshrouds
the crimson beauty, then vanishes
into the tulip's mouth.
I cannot say how long
he kneels before my bus
pulls to the curb, and I climb
aboard. Riding on Independence,
I glance back on all I know
of this block. The Capitol
grows larger, and as I search
the pale walls, search
for stones that fade and chip,
the night lights open up
and disclose the city's ruins.

CYNTHIA LINVILLE

No Exit

This is a place where even the invisible need a passport
a place where palm trees with purple auras
are as common as broken beer bottles
a place where everyone has a suitcase full of dirty clothes

a place where no one looks twice at a man
flapping his arms, cawing at crows
where no one looks twice at a woman
singing to bulls, herding goats no one else can see.

This is a place where a man can count up his things in peace
flat tire, torn blanket, broken string
a place where a woman can call out to the angels in dulcet tones
can quietly horde all of her worry bones.

This is a place where we become bored by our fears
where even the Devil has become passé
a place where shaky lost dogs make the best friends
a place where ravens keep us company all day.

MARJORIE MADDOX

Between States

Twenty miles into Ohio,
sky shifts downward,
opens wide to hide hills,
pries the "hi" from the sides of its name.
There a man sits in the middle of his life
at the end of a long, asphalt driveway.
He is waiting for Ohio to stop smiling,
blows smokey O's into its O's,
turns his hometown face away.

Old enough to recognize a con,
he still wants to be wrong,
favors the fake friendship,
the grinning fields.

Where is the river's rich voice
to argue him home?
The unstrange land in the stranger?

Too long the dandelions—
cavalier and convinced they are carnations—
two-stepped to his door,
saluted each entrance and exit;
too long the cardinal flapped furiously
away at his hello.

He fingers fallen buckeyes,
their blind eyes overlooking
what he's lost, then aims
toward some imaginary boundary
that even now turns beautifully
at the edge of the dead field
into another world
not here.

J. H. MARTIN

Un Autre

Another day
another city

filled with
more people
more buildings
more cars
more madness

all glimpsed through the windows
of this spy's hungover eyes

It could be
London,
Beijing,
Rangoon or Rome

It doesn't matter at all

Everywhere's the same
when you're alone and lost
in this crowded mind—

alive
yet dead
to all of these forms—

shaped by the light
of plastic perceptions

stained by the smog
of an impulsive desire

to understand all of these things
which can never be understood

either today or on any other given day

in this virtual world
which neither exists nor does not exist

as it passes through me and I pass through it.

CATHERINE MCGUIRE

Squatter's Flag

The time dwindles, the year dissolves—
rain stirs the ivy leaves
as Portland's steady drizzle spoils
its eighteenth day. The hills
hold snow like heavy cream, but here
frozen mud and dead leaves
are worn away, cell by cell,
their passage imperceptible,
like seconds in a fading year.

The highway spins off-ramps like fraying cord
lashed to the grid of streets.
Under bridges, citizen phantoms
weave fragments and slag into fragile cocoons.
Extruded cinder blocks anchor beds,
bags; possessions that the winds covet.
Sulfurous street lamps pierce the shadows,
waxing robust on hollow cheeks.
No one stands straight here.

As headlights strafe black plastic walls,
they burst upon the Flag: vivid
red/white bars cross girders, a square of deep starry night,
a staunch barrier to cold, rain,
and godless communism. By morning
it is gone—someone objects
to free PR for Liberty;
someone rejects bright colors
in a graveyard. Or something.

JAMES B. NICOLA

The Sack Man and the Suitcase

Santa Claus, we called him.
He reigned on a Bryant Park
northside bench
for years. I'd jog, he'd wave,
and I'd wave back.
And many spoke to him.
The year he disappeared
with all his sacks
a guard told me he'd found city housing.
We'd called him Santa Claus, although he'd worn no red.

*

I've started jogging at pier 84.
There's a long wooden dock
over the Hudson, new this year,
not too bad for the back or the knees.
Last month I saw a suitcase on wheels
locked to a temporary chain link fence.
The next week, saw it again. No person.
Whose was it?
Did I recognize the face who'd been there,
among all the strollers and sitters,
both times?
It was attached with a bicycle lock
so maybe the owner wasn't around.
Though he should be careful, what with security and bomb scares and all.

*

Then only two weeks ago I saw it being wheeled by
a dangerous dark character in a black-and-blue sweat suit.
The first time, two weeks earlier, he'd been sleeping
on a bench, I think I recall.
I do not merely notice him this time, though: I nod.
His face is muscular, sleek, and ignores everything.

*

Last week, on my arrival, same sweat suit.
I say Hey, and almost wave. His eyes are open
but the rest of him ignores me, glistening darker in the sun.

*

The other day I get there, I'm twenty yards from him.
He's listening to 1010 WINS. I figure
he's no Santa Claus holding court.
And he looks up, face lit, and waves at me!
I was ready to ignore him, but smile, salute, and jog.
There are Asian fishermen
who tend three lines and catch crabs, gathering crowds.
We applaud each catch.

*

Today the suitcase man, not Santa Claus,
holds the net for them, it's on a long pole. I clap
at the first catch of the day, just after dawn.
I don't know anyone's name but several speedwalking couples
wave now, as does the suitcase man.

*

We have become New York.

*

I don't know if I should ask the suitcase man
if he knows about all the lists he could get on
for city housing.
You don't want to be presumptuous, but you do want to help.
Maybe next week we'll engage in conversation.

And I wonder where Santa Claus is now
and if he's happy
and would he like to talk to the suitcase man.

SCOTT OWENS

Leonard

Leonard sleeps in the field
next to the hardware store
his family owns. They've tried
to take him in, but he won't go
anymore, unwilling to abide
by their rules, no booze,
no women, you have to take a bath.
Every now and then his brother,
the mayor, puts him up in a hotel room,
or takes him back to rehab,
but he never stays for long,
preferring the outdoors
and the conversation of people
mostly in their right minds.

There's nothing scary about him,
just a harmless drunk, though
at times the smell can put you off.
He wasn't beaten as a child,
no one abandoned him
or locked him in closets.
No one exposed him to anything
he shouldn't have seen.
Despite it all, he's pleasant enough
to talk to, and he knows about everything
there is, people, sports, celebrities,
all the latest news, everything
except how he got here and why
most days he wouldn't be anywhere else.

SCOTT OWENS

Meadow: Mary and Joseph

Tired, dead tired, head ringing
with unending questions.
Here, beside this stone,
in the shadow of these trees, lie down.
Rest. I'll kneel beside you and wait.

Who cropped this field, miles
from anywhere? What hand? What foot
cleared this path before us? What
unfathered God lay down this road?
Damned light. Damned voices. Damned city
I go to for this unearthly making.

How alone I feel, and betrayed.
Unhoused, unwifed, unallowed
to do what any man would do.
No child to call my own,
cuckold, outcast, nothing but these
strong-armed angels filling my head,
pushing their happy consequence
of miracles. What do they know
of doubt, shame, emasculation.

To be so chosen, stem of Jesse,
rod of Abraham. Am I reduced
or risen? Father, son, and
holy escort, chauffeur with donkey,
steward to God's great anomaly,
seedless, fruitless, bearer of this
living cross. Will I hold him?
Will I cry at his inevitable hanging?
What father will he cry out for?

Unborn prince of unlikely blood,
playing insane games of a Greek god,
what heavenly bliss will this bring me?

Yours is not the only sacrifice
to be made here. What manhood, what life,
what father's hand is severed and replaced?

Sweet, angelic face, near death
in this quiet perfection,
you can't imagine the doubts I've had.
What hands are these to tear and rend?
Some things weigh heavier only because
they have to. How much these eyes
can't see. *Rest. Rest. Rest.*

CONNIE POST

Extremities

You can lose body parts
crossing a city street

you can lose your hands
inside the outstretched arms
of a woman's cardboard sign
disappear inside another country

you can lose your feet
inside the tap dancer's shoes,
the click, click, click on the pavement
a way to measure the world
as it falls away
in incremental eight counts

you can lose your skin to the wind
it finds the exact place where
your pores are most open

you can lose your organs
as they carefully fall outside of you
while you step into a cross walk

you can lose your brain as the pigeons
fly over you
as the taxi cab runs too close to the curb
and never understand why you were built
like this
barely sustainable
commanded to stay whole
while stepping over
your swollen self

as if all those pieces you've
picked up along the way
were never you

CONNIE POST

Your Doorstep

If a man comes to your front door
with a burlap sack
and tells you your fate is inside
believe him

believe him only if his eyes are mottled
with the shades of your secrets

don't tell him about the last time
you dropped your fork at the dinner table
the way it sounded like remorse

don't tell him how much time
you spend searching
for olives or cloves of garlic
when September turns to stone

don't tell him how you fill your flimsy cloth bag
with figs and orchards of aligned sorrow

or that you have hidden your mother's
recipes in the shed behind your life

don't even tell him that your mouth
has sought the water from the bottom of an old well
or admit that at night
your lips remain slightly parted
like mercy or soft ground

look away from his disheveled shoes
beg him to leave the sack closed
If only for now

ask him for a broken clock,
another basket of olives

then sit down together

tell him you are hungry

he will understand

SARAH RUSSELL

Urban Sovereign

Gaunt, in a grimy dress and Burger King crown,
she occupies the median
with timely crayon-scrawled edicts:
    "Happy Spring" in April,
    "Whew, it's Hot" in August,
    "Boo" at Halloween.

From Lexus comfort,
drivers proffer coins through half-closed windows
that she grabs, stone-faced,
with yellow rubber kitchen gloves.

I drive on wishing she had a cape.
A cape would solve everything.

PAUL SALUK

End Game

Face down
on the baking sidewalk,
he was a place in time forever
set outside their minds.

Like a herd parts to avoid a carcass,
each day they move
around him

and no one
would know
the chill of the boil—

day by day
hour by hour
cooking him
sunny side down.

J. J. STEINFELD

Until the Paperwork Is Done

no identification was found
his pockets empty
emptiness a puzzling foretelling
no one claimed the body
and computer checks
turned up only a few possibilities
of this male in his mid to late seventies
but they wound up being
fruitless as the tree he was found under
in the heart of downtown
if downtown can have a heart

one worker in the morgue
who whistled while he worked
told another
who hadn't yet learned true pitilessness
people go missing all the time
people disappear and reappear
with new names and saddened faces
and not just in the movies
some wind up dead

he had a life, left footprints
everyone leaves footprints
the younger worker says
forgetting for a moment
that he's not supposed to care
about the unidentified, the empty pocketed

the seasoned worker
boasts he will have a beautiful gravestone
the best money can buy
when his time comes
the other says he will be cremated
and have his ashes thrown into the air

in the heart of downtown
near the tree where they found this old-timer
and he puts the body away
until the paperwork is done

WALLY SWIST

Amputee, Miami, 1959

He clutches brown-bag Thunderbird
beneath the shade of the Woolworth's

awning, spread like a pelican's wing.
His casters grease the pavement with a slick

roar that stops us as cold as a ball bearing.
Women scrape heels where his knuckles grind,

as they walk by, self-righteous and suburban
in tight sweaters. Our shock eye to eye

is the glazed stare of dead fish, our barracuda
nightmares, Key West shark attacks.

His cart's path in the dust is a trail
of loose ribbons, palm fronds, his holy spirit.

Hibiscus, I hear him say, *I just want
to dip my legs in clear water.*

SHERRE VERNON

Why You Walk Alone

What is sin but warm milk, cardamom
    and a little paper; every few years
    a pair of new boots?

Walking, of course, hurts: truck fumes
    grating the nostrils, the weight
    of your head, heavier for always looking

        to the highway. But this way
        you can touch the yellow crawl of chaparral
        scratch, in length, a bit of styrofoam.

It should hurt, though, for all it yields:
    the few hours you speak to no one
    but yourself, imagining

        how you will cut off the cuff
        of your jeans, rather than wash
        them again; just how you'd shade

        the steel bench if you had
        the right pencil, or verbs—
        if you were an artist at all.

LILLO WAY

11th and Pine

This corner is no picnic,
no pocket park, no pea patch,
no Japanese garden of cherry trees
blinking blossoms onto the backs
of koi outfitted in gold lamé robes.

This corner's got *Queers in Space,*
Hoes on Rollerblades, Anal Cunts
with Strong Intentions sidetracked
straight up the wall of a warehouse
which ships and receives and provides
parking for its customers: bottle cap,
candy wrap, cigarette pack, molding snack—
parked not between the lines.

On this corner are bone-crossed bleeding needles,
infected palimpsested poster paper puke
from months and years of stapled *Cops in Capsules,*
stapled *Pussy Punks in Purple.*

A man in a night black sweater lies flattened face down
in the outerspace green of cornered astroturf.
He is sleeping. Or dead. He is tired.
Or drunk. He has had a heart ache.
Or a heart attack. He's playing possum.
He just can't take it anymore.

On the other side of a grime-trashed loading ramp
an ungrown boy fetalizes
around his new suede sneakers,
a skinscraper sandpaper skateboard
pillow under his narcotized cherub cheek.

I am standing over this cherub boy,
above this black-night man, begging
to hold in both my hands a wand
of transmundation to transport them

into transparent beds in a house of hearts
where the man takes on the electric blue
of the last midnight sky,
where the boy's marigold hair
stocks his head with ponds of golden fish.

RICHARD WIDERKEHR

Homeless

You want a warm coat for your grief.
On Railroad Avenue, you stop me
and ask, "Don't I know you?
Didn't you once sing that song?"

No, but I wonder.
And the closet you hid in
up on the unit, scared of the voices—
was that you, also?

April, in its thin rags,
has stopped asking for spare change.

Friend, do I know you?
Today a street. Tomorrow a star.

METAMORPHOSIS

Writings About Aging

PEGGY AYLSWORTH

Giving Thanks

Despite the gray heads
                        the jazz goes on.
My ears are less.
                 My knees need grease,
   but the mellow sax
                      delivers me
from evil
                          closer to the sun
     without a comet
                 to ride.
Growing old is a privilege
                       though...
   well, the wheelchairs,
                        the walkers.
No need for a church,
                 a synagogue.
   Faith it is own vehicle
                       without a license plate.
Even the cab
           keeps its motor running
                  and the cucalyptus tree
    bends lower
              every year.

NINA BENNETT

Déjà Vu

We sit on the deck, sip red wine,
watch girls prance across the dance floor,
gyrate to the thumping bass.

I pick at the crab dip, ask the waitress
for more pita chips, remark
on the sunset, yawn.

You sigh, grimace as you shift
your bad hip in the resin chair,
stare at the yachts docked in the marina.

We were those girls.
We squeezed firm cheeks
into crayola colored denim,

teetered through night clubs
on three inch heels, left trails
of posh perfume.

We slammed shots at the bar,
tossed long, straight hair,
trolled the band, danced

through last call. Your
cinnamon strands flashed
purple under disco lights.

We were young, hip,
hot. I swear we were.
We were them.

MARION BROWN

Subway

No longer sure-footed now that I
answer to Madam or Ma'am
and a burly man gets up from his seat

and sweeps the air clean with his hand,
I clutch the pole, sit, and interrogate
the face I just put on.

What makes today too much to stand—
dark circles, little makeup or
too much, the hard light underground?

A gallant offer tips me from my own
two boots and takes me down. Only
the tall stranger knows. I console myself,

he thinks you have a long way to go.
The riders lurch in their places, speeding
as they sit or hang from the bar. Call me

a fool for manners, but a gentle gesture
ought to be acknowledged, no matter how
sour on the bench I hurtle into the dark.

DAVID CHORLTON

Night Thoughts

> It's Tuesday
> and my urine flows freely
> to the end of time
>
> —Suzanne Stapeley

Suzanne lives at the Villa Ocotillo, Scottsdale, Arizona,
where the other residents distrust her
writing. Each Friday she comes to class
carrying a loose leaf binder full
of fantasies, confessions, and details
only her doctor should know.
She's not afraid to tell how she feels

when Juan, the waiter, brushes against her
before serving Jello
or to recall the secrets of a Happy Hour
that kindles passions for which
the fuel is running low. Her latest lover
is Saddam Hussein. He's dark,
mysterious, and nobody else likes him.
Suzanne cares more about his eyes

than politics. When the buffet has been cleared away
and all there is to drink
is an ice cold Coke at 2 AM
she cannot sleep, and spins a thread
of longhand script
to state, *I'm eighty-two years old
and there's nothing
I can't say now.*

CARL CHRISMAN

Our Evenings

Our overgrown evenings
Turn to old mirrors in the morning,
The dead man looking back says nothing.
Our conversations are sometimes
Merry-go-rounds, pure sensation.
Other times they become card games,
Quips between the next move
Or card tricks where only certain illusory cards
Are remembered.

BETH COPELAND

Keeping Time

He dozes in the blue wheelchair,
opening his eyes when I enter his room.
He smiles. Does he know me?

Maybe. Or maybe he just sees
a resemblance to my photograph
pinned to the corkboard on his wall.

At 94, he sleeps almost all day,
drifting in and out of dreams, distant
time zones and long forgotten memories.

We look at photographs in *National Geographic*,
snowflakes, maple leaves, and stars magnified
thousands of degrees. I glance at the clock,

wondering if I should stay or leave.
His watch is lost. He forgot where he left it.
It's here somewhere still keeping time.

When I was small I'd climb into his lap.
He'd hold his watch to my ear, the gold
warm from his wrist, as I listened to

minutes ticking, believing he could hold
time in his hands forever, a heartbeat
that would never stop.

JAMES CROTEAU

Cover Boys

    (In appreciation of Walt Whitman's "We Two Boys Together Clinging")

Each June yields his boyish grin,
his familiar smell of summer sweat
and well-tilled soil, my lover's harvest
adds to our table, his hands hold
sturdy stalks of green, paler
than the earthy headed horde
of fine florets. We clean and chop
this first crop, as we have each year
for thirty-six. The pot sets to boil,
steam fills the air with souvenirs—

we were once two boys together
clinging, I was there at his first
sight of ocean, we pledged in public
when marriage was a far horizon.
For all life vigils we've held hands—
when time necessitated the vet's needle,
free hands on fur, we bid farewell.
Two boys by the sea, cover photo
for our album, almost filled, near forty years,
now we take pills with morning coffee,
two men aged together. The ring
of the kitchen timer, we do not cling,
turn off the burner, not much left to do

before we eat, add a pinch of salt,
and a touch of butter. Half-a-smile,
half-a-joke, my lover says: *Picture us
on the cover of* The Advocate
or Out Magazine: Two old men
at their kitchen counter, bowed
over bowls of broccoli,
essential nutrient, home-grown.

ANTHONY DIMATTEO

Assistive Learning

They share the camaraderie of death,
the lonely bruise that cannot heal,
the stitch that makes them friends,
provokes anxious laughter and grants
the sleep that keeps them from despair.
This is their private reward and wisdom,
not wanted by those too busy or afraid
to sit down at their table and listen.

HEATHER DOBBINS

Lunch Hour in the Nursing Home

I rub her arms with lavender lotion
because I can't sit still, a busybody
like she was. Her bracelet fits mid-arm,
its plain metal with my mother's phone number
etched in it. She holds my hand to her mouth
as we listen to Bach's *Brandenburg Suites*
and asks, "Are you here now?"
The rest is mumbled memory, an unheard
smudge in a room where I chew gum
so I don't taste the smell when I leave.
At work, I help an Asperger's boy
write a paragraph about Disco Bear,
a character in his screenplay.
He says to me, *No offense,*
but you smell like my grandmother's house.

HEATHER DOBBINS

P-H-E-N-O-M-E-N-O-N

When my grandfather came home,
he weighed eighty pounds. The Red Cross
fed doughnuts to the prisoners of war,
exploded most of their stomachs.

The next time we thought he'd die, I was 11.
I had just won a spelling bee. The winning word
was *phenomenon*. To survive several strokes.
He said, *Then you can help me remember words.*

The last time, I held his hand after making Mamaw
go to the cafeteria. I knew he could not die
with her in the room. How do you spell
the lies I told him so he could leave us?

BONNIE DURRANCE

Mother is Coming

Last stop
On a long train
She won't like the hotel.

Let's start papering the walls
Of heaven for her
No mirrors facing west.

In the garden of immortals
Peaches ripen
She will want meat.

She paces at night
Telling the black and white dog on the pillow
How she was meant for a life on the stage.

There she is, young and pretty
At the kitchen window crying
While my father stabs at his plate

And we stir our peas in silence.
She says the marriage was a role of a lifetime
Worthy of an Academy Award.

This new role will be harder.
How will she know herself
In the world of the shadow people

Bent over their walkers
Stepping careful in slippers
On the way to the dining room.

BONNIE DURRANCE

My Mother in John Muir's Wood

She, who never wore blue jeans
Is wearing white sneakers
And holding my arm.
The ground is uneven.
This walking together
Is new to us.

She says, pointing upwards
Look at those trees!
Take a picture of that one!
I say I've heard redwoods
Have no program for dying
She keeps stepping forward

Still gripping my arm.
She's not thinking of death.
She says, Look! How the young trees
Grow up from the mother trunks.
She says she wants to read up on redwoods
And maybe get a book on John Muir.

So, cradled in imaginary timelessness
We go together toward the light
Of the gift store
Breathing with the waves of the redwoods
Moving together
Towards all that comes after.

LAURA FOLEY

Ode to My Feet

For years I've thought them queer,
hiding them
in steamy boots and sneakers,
but recently, I've begun to like
their well-worked lines, blue
veins, tapered, skinny elegance.
Funny looking, yes, oddly
protuberant, awkwardly angled,
unlike anyone else's,
models for a medieval statue's,
ancient granite feet
on a church facade,
thoroughly unmodern.
Yet, how well they climb steep cliffs,
work my slinky kayak's rudder,
how they tingle, tapping to music
across a wooden floor,
dangling below me
when I sit on high seats,
and turning pink as we wade
the cool mountain pond,
warming, as they carry me
faithfully home to rest.

TAYLOR GRAHAM

Father, Son

Only one lamp to define the room
that holds him, small
as every thing trembling in his hand.

The other brings his separately
grown knowledge, orders
of arrangement, intent. Is it enough

to spark an evening meeting—
fumble-friction over crumpled papers,
old drafts, misfiring nerves—

this figure contracted into a loose
robe wrapped about for
warmth? Call it the cold season

of miracles. Might they forget them-
selves, the words stern or
mumbled, obscure to-and-fro into

a new order, a meeting. Clothed
in boundary, but the mind
fluid. Lamplight flows between.

KAREN GREENBAUM-MAYA

Dignitas

The taxi driver knows the way.
A moat marks the house you've come for.
Koi flirt away when you cross.
The bed is safe in a far corner.

A moat marks the house you've come for.
Pomegranate-red blanket, ice-white sheets:
the bed waits, safe in a far corner,
when you know each day too well.

Pomegranate-red blanket, ice-white sheets.
The house looks away from the city
where you know each day too well,
where the good hours are all used up.

The house looks away from the city.
Your life savings buy you nothing
when the good hours are all used up.
Pay the fare, leave a good tip.

Your life savings buy you Nothing,
the coin to float you across.
Pay the fare, leave a good tip.
The taxi driver knows the way.

KAREN GREENBAUM-MAYA

Birdie...

...her nickname, from the German Berthe,
bones gone porous as a sparrow's,
knees and ankles bowed
by eighty years of marketing and cooking.
By ten I had to bend down to kiss her.
I prowled her apartment
with its icebox you could open from outside,
closets jammed with mysteries,
visitors' boxes of picked-over chocolates,
hexagon tiles in the bathroom
and her smell, of face powder and old pipes.

Summer mornings she'd totter in early,
fresh off the bus from the Fairfax farmers' market,
balancing flats of blueberries, strawberries.
She'd spend the day frying crepes for blintzen,
filled each one so full, the crepe breached
and the strawberries wilted and fried.
I favored the flat side where the crepe was doubled,
crispy and chewy like the potstickers I hadn't tasted yet,
and soft and gently sweet besides.

Suddenly she wasn't safe in the kitchen.
Her hands didn't know anymore
where the knife's edge was,
so she resorted to bean sprouts, already in strips,
bologna, hardly needing cooking
to reach that chewy dark brown edge.
But the stove's constant heat was sly
and got away from her,
only just once, then every time.
We stood around her, helpless, silenced
like big dumb fledglings,
while she snarled and wept at us,
our insolence,
our wanting to cook for her.

NANCY GUSTAFSON

On the Edge

I'm on the edge of Old,
    the cutting edge I'd say,
the edge that takes the butter knife
    to cut the fat away
and leaves the lean upon the plate
    to eat for lunch that day.

I'm lately urged by friends:

    "Pursue a new career.
It's time to start to school once more,
    begin anew, my dear.
Don't dare to rest, or worse,
    plop in a rocking chair.
Get up! aerobics class
    begins today at nine.
Take aspirin for the pain and jump
    your brains out one more time.
Clean the house and cook a meal,
    invite your friends to dine;
curl your hair, wear rouge
    to mask the ravages of time."

Forget it! lose the mask,
    let wrinkles out to play.
With coffee mug, in thread-bare robe
    I'll read a book all day,
or walk with my old friend, the dog,
and watch the crazy neighbors jog.

NANCY GUSTAFSON

Aunt Saphrana Counsels

When she was forty-five
and I was twenty-three,
Aunt Saphrana counseled me:
    In life, if you resolve to win
    you must toughen up your mind.
    Profit from that stubborn chin,
    straighten up that curvy spine.
    Stand unbendable on a pedestal
    to achieve what life has destined.
    Stick to the rules immutable,
    wear tenacity like a garland.
        If you want to reach your goals,
        let no one obstruct your road.

Now I am sixty-one
and she is eighty-three,
Aunt Saphrana counsels me:
    Abandon the conceit of isolation,
    in your scars discover power,
    in fellowship find consolation,
    accept the thorn that guards the flower.
    Imagine life as light through crystal,
    leap into the human stream,
    burn your scratchy hermit's mantle
    and seek the joy that each day brings.
        Hold hands along the stony path
        and when you stumble, laugh.

LOIS MARIE HARROD

The Widow Laments Another Autumn

He planted trees
to make new this world—
as many as our plot
could bear.

For he was that kind
of man, one who
husbanded his acorns
against the sky descending.

Seed against sorrow,
he said, shade to cool
the warming woe.
The little we can do.

But he did not
foresee the fall out
of his un-wiving—
the thousand leaves.

Unsweatered and bare-armed
I rake and rake.
I do not know why
I live so long.

KAREN PAUL HOLMES

She Sat Alone in a Red Sequined Sweater on December 20

It was Ruby Tuesdays in the mall after church.
I'm sure my 86-year-old mother chatted
too much
to the kind waiter who listened.

As Mother reports on the phone,
she enjoyed *that oh-so-tender Petite Sirloin,*
the best baked potato,
and a *Triple Layer Brownie*
the waiter chose for her.

When I asked for the check, he said
the young couple in the next booth had paid!

I tell others...Mother tells others...
others tell others.... When the story goes around,
I'd like to think hundreds of widows
will have been treated to lunch.

I want to fly to Florida, track down
those strangers, pump their hands, hug their necks,
buy them groceries for the rest of their lives.
Instead, I have to imagine their eyes
meeting across the table, conspiring,
Let's buy her lunch.

Maybe they held hands, and yes,
thought of their grandmothers: round faces
with deep smile lines, making the most
of a meal alone in red sequined sweaters
and black brimmed hats.

PAUL HOSTOVSKY

Pearl in Bubble Wrap

She's pretty deaf and pretty blind and pretty
in an octogenarian sort of way, her hair completely
white, and pulled back tight from her high smooth forehead.
If staring at the blind is rude, I must be downright
scurrilous. Scurrilous piety, this kneeling down in front of
her wheelchair, to tie her shoelace which has come untied,
then sitting back down in the seat across from her
to stare some more. Snap, snap, snap, goes the bubble wrap
in her mottled fist, her fingers thirsting after the next
and the next explosion under thumb. I can see on her face
how sensual, how satisfying this sensation is for her
whose sensations are mostly tactile now that she's pretty
deaf and pretty blind and pretty alone here at the nursing home
where they can't communicate with her. So they give her
the bubble wrap, lots of it, to keep her busy, happy, maybe even
joyful, bursting joy's grape over and over, getting her
eighty-year-old ya-ya's out in her wheelchair parked
in front of my eyes. And I can't help wondering
how much bubble wrap she's gone through in the days
and weeks and months she's been here, how many miles of it
she's consumed. She's probably been to the moon and back
on her fingertips, dancing along the backs of these plastic
turtles, leaping across these disappearing stones, these rivers
of bubble wrap, oceans of bubble wrap. "Pearl!" I shout
into her left ear, the one with the cochlear implant. "I have
to get going now!" She looks up vaguely, pauses briefly from
the pursuit of more pleasure in her lap. I give her a kiss
and head for the elevator. Once inside, I push the Lobby button
several times before it lights up. Then I worry the Braille beside it
with my index finger, all the long way down to the street.

ANN HOWELLS

Mom and Pop

When she was pregnant and money
scarce, she wore his shirts from junior high,
ones stuck at the closet's back.
Today his drum set molders in the attic;
guns, twenty-years unfired,
stand at attention inside the safe,
and 1983's hiking boots still serve—
waterproofed each season,
insoles added, leaks filled with bathtub caulk.
When they eat Mexican,
he chooses flautas, again,
while she scours the menu.
If it's Chinese, he orders broccoli beef
while her nose presses the glass
evaluating each possibility.
At breakfast he says: two eggs, over easy,
sausage patties, not links,
wheat toast in place of biscuits.
She peruses selections:
omelets, hot cakes, waffles—
worlds unfold before adventurous tastebuds.
He grows, incrementally, mired,
looks back, as she strains forward.
Twin moons, they circle the homestead,
never meeting.

A. J. HUFFMAN

Aging in an Instant

Mirror.
Silver surface.
Keeper of self-image.
Plane reveals echoing touches
of time.

A. J. HUFFMAN

My Body is Turning Against Me

Each month expels all but arid spots
where once a raging river flowed, a bitter
reminder that the red of my biological clock
has twisted to grandmother mahogany.
In this stage, the bells still chime, but
no one really cares. Admirers have moved
on to the newer models—cuckoos,
it seems, are all the rage now.

I look in the mirror and see the grain
of forty years—barely
visible. I smile and retreat to the corner
I am being forced to fill,
knowing that antiques are still coveted by some,
and worth more when they appear to be still
in mint condition.

A. J. Huffman

My Bladder is Shrinking

with age, though to be fair, I have
never slept through the night.
That I cannot blame on bodily functions, but
nights that used to be filled
with restless ramblings, endless tossings
and turnings are now broken
into dozens of segments, each punctuated
by the necessary tinkling, urine
dripping into porcelain bowl.
I cannot go
more than two hours without
a bathroom break. My kidneys act
as alarm clock, scream for release. I pry
my head from pillow, zombie-walk
through dark maze of bedroom and hallway,
fumble for light
switch and uncooperative lid
to expel the liquid I stopped
consuming at 6:00 p.m.

JOSEPH HUTCHISON

First Bird at First Light

The trilling of your solo
piccolo flows like the cool

well water dad pumped
into the zinc bucket I held

up for him, out behind
our rented log cabin

in a breezy aspen grove.
Where, I wonder, was

that grove, that cabin,
that creaky iron pump?

Each day at dawn
your song calls back

that moment of flurried
sun and shade—and I

wonder. But then,
as just now, you stop,

and however hard I listen,
the sky begins to brim

with a pitiless brightness,
and the past melts back

into a maze of trees,
taking its secrets with it.

ROBERT S. KING

Mirror at the Speed of Light

The mirror moves faster than I do,
ages me ten years per day,
makes faces I've never seen,
tries to frame me
but can't decide how I should look.
I get smeared by the speed of its light.

If I play imposter and close the blinds,
it might jump to dark conclusions,
that I am solid, not a streak of gray.
If I pose in loose fits,
it can't see stretch marks on my belt,
can't see the gray alien
with light years in his eyes.

The mirror clock runs backward.
Its hands don't shake like mine;
but like mine, they never come to rest.

Yet through that glassy hole,
the clock points to a point of light.
I see myself coming to myself,
even as the reflection no longer mimics
who I think I am.

ROBERT S. KING

The Light Sedative of Dark

The measured clap clap of my teaspoon on the table
awaiting my dose and the do-not-drive warnings
to easy-chair me into re-runs and the dim hum
of test patterns, multiple choice game shows
with each answer wrong, innovative boredom,
black and white documentaries on the private lines of aging,
indecipherable waves on cables and satellites
whirring on their wrinkling orbits.

So I give myself to the gray light of sleep,
my dream on its back like a crocodile luxurious to
the tummy-rubbing therapeutic masseuse.

I remember before we are born we say goodbye,
hold our noses and dive into this cold medicine called breath.
The sun turns us darker all our lives.
We look for rhyme and find but one,
womb and tomb,
the only rift between them a waiting room.

ROBERT S. KING

Prescriptions for Two

Months without surprise visits,
my companion is a pill large enough
to choke me but not the lungs' carcinoma.
Shall I take the prescribed drowsy hope
and nod away the day? Or shall I walk the floor,
wide awake with pain, with my lover,
the oxygen tank, in tow?

Either way, you stand behind me in a photograph.
Our bed sags on my side alone now.
A bookmark stays where you fell asleep.
A brush lies tangled up with your chemo hair.
The label says your last prescription just expired.
Your perfume makes me gasp with memory.

Like a snake I work the pill down my throat
and coil up into dream. May the knock at my door
come to take my breath away.

ROBERT S. KING

Strategy for Longevity

My drive speeds up to 65,
each year faster.
The curves straighten out.
An old wind is at my back,
racing a clock no longer
running in circles.

I try to brake and detour
from the straightaways,
take the clock's hand in mine,
holding it to the best of times.

Time now is in a hurry,
closes my loopholes, flings
me further down the road.
Shifting into reverse,
I almost cheat the future
by driving backward
as far as I can go.

JUDY KRONENFELD

Her Vacated House

The mirrors are sheeted.
The chairs and couches
lose their shapes under heavy
covers. Dust congregates
in corners. She is silent
and expressionless
as a dressmaker's model.

But I need little—a door
for entry, a window, however
smeared, for light. I sit
on the draped cushions. Motes swirl
and eddy in wan shafts
of sun warming the rooms
that seem to stir. I pin
remnants, vestiges,
traces to her frame.
A long time, now,
I have been
both ventriloquist
and dummy.

I am accustomed
to the squares of my afternoons,
the *tableau vivant*
at their centers. When they tell me
the house is death's
eminent domain,
I shut my ears.
Windows shine
and windows darken; curtains fill
with light, then flatten. The glow
and shadows on her face
make me dream
she's home.

JUDY KRONENFELD

At the YW Indoor Spa

The water is happy
to see them as a dog
with a warm tongue licking
their toes. It is humble,
laving swollen
feet. Chrysoprase green,
semi-opaque, it bobbles
zipper scars on knees
as they descend—
sideways sometimes, clinging
to the rail, leaving behind
walkers and canes. Rising higher,
it willingly embraces their billowy waists,
their spines, and they sigh,
and briefly close their eyes.

Lily leans into the walking
breast-stroke with which they
begin—nippleless in her
maillot, cropped hair
glistening.

From Janet's upper arms raised high
depends an eagle cape of thick
loose flesh—soft
as feathers—mottled, dimpled,
swaying.

Carol's loose suit greyed with use
reveals a swath of pendulous white
belly or pale groin
as she swings her leg open,
closed, open, closed, knee
bent, in the "creaky gate."

On the deck, one of their granddaughters
idles, sliding down in her chair,
the air practicing caresses
as she stretches out her gold
limbs, the hollow of her throat
filling with invisible nectar.

The women in the spa
in their little purdah of no
care—salty as their own
blood—cruise, they ski
(cross-country), they rock
like the nursery horses of their
childhoods, they laugh
about who's been bumped
on *Dancing with the Stars.*

LORI LAMOTHE

Gray Sisters to Perseus

The twilight smells like moths.
Moths and libraries and children's breath
preserved in formaldehyde.

It's in our hair and our cloaks reek of it.
Everywhere the years have accumulated in layers
like the stale smoke of magic.

Nothing glows. Forget youthful ex-
foliation, alchemical regeneration.
Here you can scrub beauty all you want,

but when you're finished the ash
fallen across the bridge of your nose
is still dull as rain.

Note that we don't really look like birds.
People just say that because
our footprints resemble the shadow

of the lightning branch. In the blur of dim,
where dawn would be, we walk the beach.
The sand is gray. The water is gray.

Of course. You might think it's monotonous.
Or, like the others, you might surmise
our shared eye makes us powerful.

Perhaps. Because what you take
for a quest to conquer evil looks to us
like the sea's hammered metal.

Also, when we recall paintings of love,
we never fall headlong into crimson
but sit around all day on our driftwood

debating the intensity of angles.

LORI LAMOTHE

Road Trip to Forever

Wind dips its quill in invisible ink
and a score of yellow notes
unravels
across the day's gray premise,
which we all know by now leads
to a logic of night, ergo, sleep.

Yet the sun still runs its fingertip
over an itinerary of light—
every tree a lit match
to lead us
through Winter's tunnel,
and on the other side Spring
      emerging
so heavy with scent each
moment seems to catch
on Time's honeycomb web.

And yes, we know by now
we're hurtling toward infinity at un-
fathomable
speeds, always
skidding on perspective's black ice,
careening from impression a
      to z
but in this land of blurred latitudes
anything seems possible.
Maybe at the end of the road
a blue silk sky opens its curtains
         to reveal

Whatever the case, along the way,
there are so many roadside stands
of indelible gestures.

LORI LAMOTHE

Red Barn in Snow

All the complications of weather
have ironed themselves out.
Now the world seems clean
as a sheet reflecting light.

It's simple things that take the most space.
Sky and sea, childhood's watercolor summers,
or the cloudless electric blue
of a mind swept clean of thought.
Loneliness, silence, wind.

At the edge of the field a red barn
stands apart in a world calved overnight.
Every other thing glows with new life.

If you press your forehead against reality
all you'll see is the breath of innocence
fogging windows of perception
and the barn, rooted in the past.

Even the barn holds onto the moment—
resists the baroque of gradual dilapidations,
the scrimshaw minutiae
of repeated losses.

Instead it stays where it always has,
not far from a row of trees
too solid for fading.

And I don't think it matters
if I tell you what type of trees they are
or the names of the dead
who thought they owned them.

I don't think it matters if, like me,
you can't look at the scene and not be certain
someday you'll find your way back
to everything you believed about love.

LINDA LOWE

Voices from Twilight Time Garden Villas

Louise

Blitzkrieg of your home. Forced out after fifty years. A child running your life. Your formerly acne-infested child, the junta of your old age. You surrender. What else is there to do? You surrender to the system for old folks, a system that corrals a lot of cows and a few old steers and puts them in a place they won't call home.

You give up driving. Too many cars on the road. Too many ways to turn. Too much of everything in the world. Surplus has gone bananas, yet there's no such thing as a comfortable shoe. All that stuff and nothing fits.

You give up knowing things. So many brain cells have said goodbye, you can only wonder, did I do something useful for the world? You stroller back to babyhood with your ripe bananas and apple sauce. You're part of the fading rainbow, "Red and yellow, black and white..." All one race now: old.

Joe

Yesterday. Got talked into one of the so-called outings they offer here. Bus of us old farts chugging down the road. Matinee I'd have named "Nonsense," followed by ten dollar macaroni known as pasta now. Al drank some wine and sat there talking to his wife, who's been dead five years. Made me think of Gracie, the night we ate spaghetti at Dino's. So nervous I got sauce on my tie. But she said *Yes.*

Lida

Some years back my house burned down, along with its pitiful history of my life in things. Sagging sofa, lace curtains drooping at the windowpanes. Pictures, pictures, and the silver tarnished, the china cracking, what linens without holes? Why keep the baby's clothes? He grew up and went to war like his friends, all of them trying to kill the Cong. Cleanest thing a person can do. Light that match and over your shoulder it goes. By the time I'd smoked a dozen Lucky's, there was nothing left to cry about.

Francine

Night after night I put up with Esther's singing to her snip of a pup, who whines. The duo from hell, I call them, what with the walls so thin here it's what they mean by anorexic. Last night, when Esther opened at one a.m. spreading the news about New York, New York, I flat lost it. I got out the cast iron skillet I brought from my old home —which is to say my home—and what a thud it made against the bedroom wall! I got just what I went after. A hole the size of that wonderful skillet I fried heaps of bacon in, most every Sunday morning, for fifty-five years.

Paul

When I died, I thought as I floated near the ceiling in the E.R., *what a way to go. Not Dr. Paul Wilson, he saved lives, but oh, Paul Wilson, he died in the arms of another woman.* Then the guys gave it one more try, and *Whoosh,* I was back. Which meant I had to face my wife. But irony is everywhere, like flu in winter, and she died on the way to see me. In my dreams she's never angry. We're thirty-five or so, in Venice last night, or was it Naples?

Doreen

I go out in the hall for a little fresh air, and there's Eva shuffling by. When I ask her where in heaven's name she's going, she says, "To the beauty parlor of course. I have a standing two o'clock."

"Well fine and dandy," I say, "But it's the wrong two o'clock."
No reply.

I've been told that Eva puts pepper on her corn flakes, but I can't say for sure. I never make it down for lunch or breakfast. Dinner gives me all the human nature I can stand.

John

It's two years now that May's been gone, but she still gets mail. Mostly of the junk sort, though sometimes there's an update from her insurance company, detailing treatments she received. Some claims they pay, some they don't. I prefer to let their reasoning join the mystery of claims.

Such as who decided during the Gold Rush that a man could stake a claim to anything? How bad should I feel when the man's undone by the black deed called claim jumping? The "jumper" gets hold of a map, a map that looks scrawled by a six year old, wads it up and stuffs it in his jeans, to be opened later, at some private moment, maybe after sex with one of the saloon girls upstairs. After all, he was going to be gone for who knew how long. He waits until she leaves to freshen up before he looks. Feeling like a man again, he quickly dresses and down he goes for a couple of shots, and orders the kitchen to fix some grub. To his horse tethered outside he hollers a version of *Hi Ho Silver.* The poor guy is just one more who's got it wrong, as he gallops off to guard like dragons did, the treasure. What he thinks is treasure.

Albert Came, Too

She is silent, peevish, her visitors talking about her, not to her. She is old, worn out, they whisper, dying, soon gone. Wrong—at least not their idea of gone. She and Albert have other plans. She closes her eyes, the people disappear. Good.

She is almost alone. Albert is with her. Folks keep saying he died long ago. Ridiculous. Albert is right there on the bed, near her feet, where he should be, more family than her blood ever was. He's wearing that dopey smile. Easy for others to assume he was simple with that smile. Wrong again. Albert is a complicated dog.

He speaks to her in English when they are alone these days. Where did he pick up English? Well, it's convenient, any way she looks at it. How else to plan this trip? Doesn't matter what people say. She's not going for the other option, not about to leave this earth. Too much left to explore. She and Albert intend to map the world. Still, she is tired...a nap.

*

She is nestled in a boat. A sailboat, the one she had as a girl. Albert always came with her when she sailed, ears flapping in the breeze, that dopey smile ablaze, sharing her gladness to be alive.

Now people are waving from the shore. She waves back in triumph. They think they are waving goodbye, that she is gone. No, she is sailing into the rest of her life. But isn't that Albert racing along the shore's edge? He's supposed to come with her.

*

She has grown so light, so small, embraced by gentle hands. Someone is cradling her tiny slick body, welcoming her, wrapping her in love and a tiny blanket. She takes a mighty breath and cries, astonished. From nearby, tentative new puppy sounds caress her ears.

In a second all will elude her, the journey from there to here. All of her before. Already she knows almost nothing, only that she is warm loved alive. And that Albert came with her.

JOHN McKERNAN

The Age Of Reason

Whenever my father looked at me he would
        whisper "Son   You are a spider web"

"Yes Sir" I replied & continued reading books
        by Nabokov on butterflies

I would often fall asleep in religion class in
        school and dream of spider webs

The teacher always let me sleep through recess

"Realism is a waste of time" she said to the
        Principal

For breakfast I looked at oatmeal and watched
        sunlight glow in the frost on the window

The first artist I ever met showed me her painting
        of a baby hummingbird wrapped in spider
        silk

In the park she showed me a butterfly in midair
        in a spider web   Its tiny abdomen pulsing

Breathing

JAMES B. NICOLA

Another vase of flowers

Another vase of flowers
in the lobby at the side
on the varnished pine shelf
on the way to our mailboxes
has appeared

A table tent next to it
patiently keeps
its inverse vigil

with a name
that the young
skate by

It's a flimsy
easily-ruffled
sentry

All the senior ladies
interrupt their business
going out or in
and manage to the counter
to adore the bouquet

They raise the table tent
to their good eye

and shake their
well-set heads

then cluck their tongues once

for they too
live alone

LYNN PEDERSEN

My Grandmother Peels Apples for Sauce

She cups the apple in her left hand, works
the blade with her right,
thumbs so callused they won't bleed
if she nicks them.
A spiral of peel sighs
into the sink.

In this room, everything is used up:
the vinyl floor—its unglued seam—
frayed holes in her canvas sneakers,
the wallpaper with its orchard
of preserved pears.

She's trained herself
for seven decades
not to want.

When I ask for a bite, it's the peel she allows—
the pots on the stove
waiting, open-mouthed.

LYNN PEDERSEN

How to Move Away

It's best to wake early, four, five a.m., while
the neighbors sleep and the moon floats
like a pearl in a pool of ink. In half-light
the empty house is less familiar, less sad—the walls
with their nail holes, the carpet—its patterns of wear,
curtains with no job to do. I sit
on my suitcase, eat powdered donuts;
a napkin for a plate, juice out of a paper cup.
Make one last check of the cupboards,
the drawers. Run my hand along
the countertops, the stair rail, trace
the walls with my fingertips, each scar
proof of my childhood, my initials
carved into the tree of this, our sixth house.

My family could write a *Handbook for Leaving*—
the way we pack up during summer solstice,
disconnect from people and places like an abrupt
shutting off of electricity. My father's convinced himself
that the unknown is always better, the way the retina sees
images upside down and the brain corrects.

                                      Here I smoked
candy cigarettes, my breath in winter passing
for smoke, pale green of my bedroom. I counted
the number of intersections on the way to school (four).
I bundle memories together, weight them with stones
like unwanted kittens drowned in a creek.

What kind of animal constantly moves?
The point of migration is the return.
We're nomads without the base knowledge
of where to find water. These moves are
like arranged marriages; economics now,
love later. Maybe it's not against nature
to move. Most of the body is no more

than ten years old and blood renews itself
every 90 days. But leaving disturbs the fabric
of a place. I'd rather stay and witness change.
My mother always wanting to plant perennials
that we never stay to see. I pour some water
on the marigolds clattering around the mailbox,
Aztec flowers of death, their strong scent
a beacon to lost souls. Then we drive away,
the blank windows like the blank eyes of
the dead, waiting for someone to seal the past with a penny.

LYNN PEDERSEN

At Forty

Pattern or absence of pattern, the way a jet flies
into blankness
yet leaves a clear trail, I expect time
to reveal an underdrawing,
hatching of shadows, some rough plan
visible through another spectrum of light.

     Once, at an ophthalmologist's office,
through an accident of mirrors, I saw the interior
of my own eye, the retina's
veins like roots or a web, and then again

ten years later, this time in an astronomy
book—galaxies, clusters of galaxies, superclusters
of galaxies strung out
strands of a cosmic web, the redness
of that image, the light extending like roots
13 billion years in every direction.

     Michelangelo could see a figure
in a block of stone, waiting to be freed.
I want his vision when I look in a mirror,
his mathematical principles for depicting space,
his ability to translate three dimensions into stone.
First I'm in two dimensions, a photograph
glued to the glass; then three—I'm somewhere between
the glass and the background. All my houses, friends
come and gone. How would he sculpt me? How far out
of the stone have I come?

The Impertinence of Ice

Route 176 absorbs the roar and agitation spinning across it; an Illinois dawn rises from harvested fields. Winter will not release its net. A huddle of willows waits, still pinioned to cryptic ground. The fall of tendrils hadn't even recognized the first signs of attack.

Grandpa George was a talented farmer, but now he names abandoned hay bales as cows; tells us again he'll paint the old farmhouse white when it thaws. We remedy the conversation with small bits of humor, deciding that it must be grenadine that makes lemonade pink.

Identity is a divergent evolution, filled with growth rings and dead branches. None of us remember well the people we used to be. Turning right on Rt. 47—potholes of black freeze, impossible to avoid. The impertinence of ice has exploded the pavement we opaquely travel upon.

JEAN QUENEAU

Terminus

These weed seeds will never
reach fertile ground
Each week I pull them
one by one from your
soft faded socks
once black and navy and brown

These days I require
strong morning light
to sort and match them
two by two for your aging legs

Is this what it comes down to
Old legs   old shoes   old feet

Like a book we've both read
we know how it ends
but still
didn't realize
it would be about us

MARY RICKETSON

Walnut

Suddenly I remember
life is hard.

One walnut tree stands
at the end of my field.
Forty years I watch. It never wanders
never moves, only sheds its leaves,
drops its weakest branches
when storms rage through the cove.

What is a woman,
but a tree that walks around?
Storms and seasons leave scars
on ripened beauty,
carve hearts in the bark
where mysteries of strength lie
in the eyes of each beholder.

No decision diverts the tree.
A tree does not worry about its fate.
Straight and tall
it stands
through all seasons.

MARY RICKETSON

Stones at Sunset

I mow around each blueberry bush,
check for fungus, culprit that stole
my crop last year. Later I'll be back,
pull out persistent inner weeds.
Plump green berries
inform me without speaking,
This could be a good year.

By fluke I found this path,
grew beyond my plans.
Familiar now, I did not grow up this way.
Fate steered me in different directions.
My caring hands encourage these berries
to give sustenance and health.

My after supper walk
rhythms my thoughts, calms my mind.
White blooms of blackberries
lead the way, then bursts of daisies
cluster under locust and barbed wire fence.
Three horses almost say hello.

I spy a neighbor's stone wall,
grey and brown random rocks,
dug from a garden one by one,
stacked with no mortar, held together
only by weight and gravity.
In this light, accidental patterns of stones
resemble the chance routine of my life.
Will gravity hold me up so well?

MARY RICKETSON

Alacrity

"Let's go with alacrity,"
you hollered to me.

Word you learned
on Monday night football.

I had to ask you precisely
what it means.

"Moving on with great speed,"
you answered to me.

Christmas comes
soon for us this year.

The puppy I gave to you as a toddler
is already an aging old pooch.

Now your clothes must
be only the latest in fashion.

Your hair is just right
and your shoes are untied.

I don't know the answers to all
of your homework today.

The nest of our home grows smaller
as the world widens for you.

Yesterday a babe, you
sat crooked in my arm.

Today you stand tall.
You come up to my nose.

The time we spend eating
cookies is priceless to me.

Your life passes by me
with too much alacrity.

KRISTIN ROEDELL

My Mother's Russian Caretaker

Last Saturday I came,
and Lidiya was feeding you strained carrots.
The world has turned round
and wrong; you fed three children
by breast and spoon.
She speaks no English
but you are all inward,

you say nothing.
Still, she speaks hands.
Bathing you, dressing you,
she is like a mirror;
however you fold and unfold

she makes origami of it.
Some days you are a crane
some days you are a blackbird,
but always she gives you wings,
still believing you
remember flight.

SUZANNE SCHON

Just Leaves

I walked on the trail
feeling my bones
more than ever.
The dogs scurried past
through the fallen color
chasing squeaks and chirps.
Perhaps I envied how
their agility and speed
matched their exuberance
when mine no longer did.
Perhaps it was just that
the familiar trail lent itself
to notions
intertwined with nature.
But I decided there, on that
autumn day, that we are
just leaves.

LUCILLE GANG SHULKLAPPER

Aging

Look at
us: here we are
in our seventh decade
wearing wrinkled love with ironed
creases.

LUCILLE GANG SHULKLAPPER

Old Woman Plays Piano

in her daughter's living room of muted
tones. It was her piano.
Her mother's candelabra tinkles as it shakes
its gold-edged glass. Never broken. Once

the music cried for her. The piano bench tilts.
She leans forward, kneads its velvet tufts,
rings its bald spots picked at by fingers
unable to reach octaves; practicing

scales from a book, still in the bench. She
inhales the lemon oil she rubbed into the
wood and grasps the dishtowel soaked
with the thinness of milk

to whiten the ivory. An upright piano. Cornered
The old woman curves her wrists and raises her
hands as though to strike the broken keys.
She waits for the music.

JUDITH SKILLMAN

Trouble

When it first founders into our lives
we don't realize how broad the swath cuts,

how rapid the flow of freshwater, a frill
growing out from under a ragged shelf.

Not that we could stop it with our myths, our
psalms, or words memorized from a clipping.

Nor could we do without it, for, like death,
it represents a bookmark, a beginning

to the nothing that follows on. The heels
on a good pair of shoes wear down gradually.

When the trouble began she wore at first
a faint glow. Then her faced greened, and later

she ballooned out of her clothes. If he had
stayed *Calamity Jane* would not be a word.

Or take illness, how it spreads from one
place to the next. Like a mishap, a pest

one would chase away if the crowd allowed.
Catharsis might be a bad thing. Instead

this hanging on every detail, harassment
by telephone, mail, and invitation.

Until the need to incommode becomes
a raison d'être. Not in a scientific way—

Pascal, Descartes, and all those French brats
meant something altogether different.

They embarked on a journey to measure
the system by which an object could be said

to be complete—inherently fitted with parts,
as light to 3-D glasses moves in a circle,

not in waves. Circular motion might be
the most dangerous bird on the island.

JUDITH SKILLMAN

The Children Grow

The youngest one's shoes have pinched her toes.
Her torso strings up to her neck from a fat tutu.
Screams, anguish over what to do next—how far
to the Emily's Studio where relief can be found for the red feet,
the swollen arches? This ballerina—such a fuss.

Hasn't she spotted, jetéd, pirouetted across floors
of sprung wood made to gleam for Pointe work, weightless
as she stood on leather toe boxes stuffed with cotton,
not minding hours of work at the barre?

The ink of her tears gets all over my dress, that sailor number
I wore to weddings for ten whole years, my waist never changing,
my figure an hourglass. The youngest's problems go on
towards infinity, where stars and suns, born from gravity,
pull at one another.

                    A nebula takes shape, and, spinning
more angstily, the gas cools to a room where the trauma
of outgrowing clothes become the norm. *Oh, I miss that leotard*,
she'll say, and what can I do except cry alongside an ancient sylph
I cushioned with my shoulder, my breast, rocking
back and forth as if a little motion might save her from the world.

CAROL STEINHAGEN

Dancing

After the memorial Hank sits on a folding chair,
a plate with half-eaten sandwich at his feet.
His wife perches to his right, balancing coffee.

The man beside him eating a cookie inclines his good ear.
Crumbs fall down his chin, over the edge of his plate
onto the maroon carpet, under passing feet.

Oh, the good times we had, Dorothy and I, says Hank.

There was a roadhouse out toward Towson
where they'd get sweetly tight and dance till all hours,
pound the creaky floor until, once, they got kicked out.

Dot and I—boy, could we do the Charleston.
We'd be all over the floor. Now I can only do this:

He crosses his hands, knee to knee, twice.
His wife points at the crumbs on the carpet.
Hank shrugs; he can't make them stop falling.

Around the buffet table voices that had murmured
grow louder. The red pepper slices and tiny carrots
are gone. Smears of dip remain on the vegetable tray.

On the piano Dorothy lives again in pictures—
stretched on a beach blanket, poised on a running board—
the beautiful girl who dances still in his stories,

who never minds the hours.
His wife clears her throat, rises.
Hank crosses his hands, knee to knee, again.

CAROL STEINHAGEN

Body Art

Contrapposto it's called, the sculpted body's pose:
left shoulder and right hip raised to draw
your eye criss-cross over the torso's curve,
the groin's swell, the left leg's thrust.

Held in a visual dance, you imagine this body
your own, forever poised to step out of marble
perfection, arched soles yet unsoiled.

After eighty years, she's achieved *contrapposto*:
left shoulder raised to draw your eye down
to the slumping right. A shirt from Myrtle Beach
drapes the cast that sculpts her arm.

Her edema-swollen hand points your eye
across the body to a gnarled foot. It could be yours.
You can see it slip off slick stairs into dark.

CAROLE STONE

Verona Park

> *By Bluewater*
> *An old angler sat.*
> —Li-Po

The lawns are green and cropped like an English park.
We retirees linger on wrought-iron benches,
lift our faces to the late afternoon sun.

The warm, almost perfect summer over,
days spent observing
mothers pushing babies in strollers,

joggers, walkers, families in pedal boats,
fishermen casting for stocked trout,
brides in strapless satin dresses posing for photographers,

kids on playground slides, swing sets
and jungle gyms, men rolling bocce balls.
Parents come with toddlers,

the way my husband and I did,
to toss crusts of bread
to the green-backed mallards among the weeds.

Dusk falling early, a slice of moon
in the sky, I see my reflection in the lake.
I'm not ready to fall in.

MERYL STRATFORD

Elegy with Backward Clocks

The clocks have fallen back.
The white clock ticking on the kitchen wall,
the antique clock in the living room.
They've fallen back as leaves fall,
as darkness falls earlier each night.
The bedside alarm with its shrill voice
and luminous face, the pocket watch,
the cuckoo clock with raucous bird
and Bavarian dancers. After the fiction
of saving daylight, we've returned to facts.
Once we rose with the sun, marked time
by its shifting shadow. Now we have clocks.
Now we have months instead of moons.
We've abandoned the fantasy that we
could save some of the daylight,
even an hour of it. That we could live
our evenings in the light of the past,
borrow light from the past to postpone
for awhile the coming of darkness.
These autumn days would last forever
if we called them by another name.

LAURENCE W. THOMAS

Aging

Study the aging,
how they forget the names
they would have had trouble with at thirty.
A sudden question confuses them
like on an examination in high school,
a poser on a quiz show.
They do well for their age like children,
praised for their efforts even when they lose
or raise eyebrows when they make mistakes.
Suffer the deliberations of those getting on;
they don't dash out between parked cars,
abuse themselves,
nor end up with unwanted children.
Help them to find ways to fill their time
like travel and gardening or bridge and good books,
without ever suggesting roller blades or bungee jumping.
If there were a war,
the oldest would remember and say it isn't worth it
or that all strikes are from ignorance
blaming the unions or management
perhaps in their unwillingness to compromise.
They complain too much that no one listens
like teenagers whose ideas are shot down untried.
Think of those advancing in years
not as prone to maladies like measles or mumps
or gaining the fortunes of others to squander,
but as those with irreversible illnesses
such as old age pensions,
senior citizen discounts,
destitution, and deaths that someone else must pay for.
Consider the successes or failures of man as guides to action,
but for the condition of the world, study the aging.

SARA TORUÑO-CONLEY

Mother's Aftermath

I am still able to speak the way I dream,
a stream of abstract, fully relevant thought.
I've only forgotten your name.

Your face is still concrete as my routine, my feeding
of the dog, the bird's chirp from the clock
above the kitchen window,

noticing the way the leaves brush
against the glass. I am still able to think of time
as linear, to remember
what I ate for breakfast, to think of breakfast
as a morning activity. I am still

able to think of love as a verb
when remembering faces, I still laugh
at the same jokes.

Yet I don't understand why the days have changed,
voices are calloused; people
move quickly as though I'm a thought to be forgotten.

The knobs on the stove have been removed.

LILLO WAY

Celestial Fantasy for Dr. Alzheimer

Will you   vague angels
with your gauze wings angels
of not-knowing beauty

bear in innocence on a foggy night
the slowly fatal present
my dead mother and aunt

giftwrapped and placed
in your transparent arms
having tied to your halos

my not-so-permanent address?

After pressing your delivery
into my hands   will you bourrée
the tips of your pointed feet

on the sprung floor of my brain?

If you spread your diaphanous gowns
and settle on my shoulders
will you whisper in my ears

the few things I need to remember?

ABIGAIL WYATT

Bluebells, An Elegy in Late Spring

We labor up the hill, the sun on our backs,
wilderness leaping on all sides
and, all about us, is the cawing of the crows
and, ahead of us, a miracle of bluebells
so that, where we tread softly, new trails open up
and their heavy-headed sweetness fills the air.
"How blue they are," you say.
"They have reached their zenith;
by tomorrow, they, too, will be fading."
You squeeze my fingers—
so much confession and forgiveness
in the sly slipping in of a word.

ABIGAIL WYATT

Everything She Said

And so it's all true, everything she said,
everything she tried so hard to tell me;
every hint and clue she laid before me;
everything I mocked and ignored:
how the world turns faster and the years flash by
in the time it takes a rosebud to open;
how dreams dwindle down to a handful of stars
and passion to a spoonful of tears.
She tried to persuade me when I was a child
to believe in the great beauty I was born with;
I could not see then beyond that glass
in which I found the monsters of my fear
but I would have her stroke my hair now
and say it is the color of September.
I would see her sorrows, strung like pearls,
and I would bow to everything she said.

ABIGAIL WYATT

Kissing Is a Young Person's Game

*(a conclusion reached by a young acquaintance on seeing
two older people sharing a passionate embrace)*

A bald statement: no ifs, no buts,
without qualification or compromise;
instead all the splendid, contemptuous certainty
of the never-to-be-dead, never-to-be-old,
callous and shallow-hearted young.

I want to take him aside, this pale,
callow youth who curls his lip in distaste,
who cannot see the gift that is his,
and who scarfs his eyes by
looking down his nose;
I want to say to him, softly
and with no hard feelings: *Listen:*
you do not understand.

Look, I want to tell him,
know how happy you should be
to see how love endures without fading:
to love deeply is a blessing
at every stage;
every age
is made precious
by a kiss.
And who scarfs his eyes by
looking down his nose;
I want to say to him, softly
and with no hard feelings: *Listen:*
you do not understand.

Look, I want to tell him,
know how happy you should be
to see how love endures without fading:

to love deeply is a blessing
at every stage;
every age
is made precious
by a kiss.

JAMES K. ZIMMERMAN

Old Letters From Myself

the pages have softened
to a vague and musty yellow

the skin of wrinkled hands

the stark blackness of ink
has mellowed to a sleepy green
or the purple shadows
     of forgotten love

but still I can recall myself
     wide open to the world
whispering between the lines
     of an uneven scrawl
in sprawling fragrant dreams
and murky pools of desolation

a ticket to a lottery before
the numbers have come up

the patina of a perfect mirror
in a dark and airless room

and still I hear the callow voice
     through misty distances
and the sallow fingers of time

reaching for what has yet to come
singing of what will never be

I am a winter window laced
with tentacles of glittering frost

OUR PLACE

Writings About the Earth

PAULA ASHLEY

Sunset Vista

I came from forsythia, hollyhocks, rain and snow
to desert heat, walls of dust, and monsoon storm.

I did not expect to stay here long. Towhees scratch
under bougainvillea and the lack of water in the local wash

leads me within myself for grace. I've climbed
Bright Angel Trail, logged the Havasupai too

but now that I'm in my seventieth
year, the Hedgpeth Hills are home.

Here a chuckwalla suns upon a basalt rock
amongst yellow desert scrub, his crimson breast,

a lover's pomegranate, on show to mates nearby.
Time has erased miles of citrus groves,

sheep stopping traffic on past commutes,
crop dusters swooping under power lines,

and Japanese flower stalls on Baseline. While today
the city brings art galleries, plenty of shopping malls,

I sit out back under my trees to watch hummingbirds
flit orange bell to orange bell, while finches perch

in the rosemary. And in the long hot desert night,
coyotes howl the haunting chant of loss.

RUTH BAVETTA

Odette on the Sand

A disturbance
of light, grey-white
as a foggy morning.
Separated

from the corps, she died
with grace,
eye falsely bright
in its hour

of blindness,
feathery tutu spread
across the sand at the edge
of the lake,

beak slightly parted
in a last cold gasp.
Quills and plumes,
the detritus of her bones,

encircle the garish
reds, blues, yellows
of ingested plastic,
encircle us.

MARION BROWN

Lament in Many Chapters for the End of the Earth and Love

i
Love runs without fuel.
No more can one turn on the switch
of day. Someday the sun will not.
Does a blink end
on an open or a closed eye?

ii
Two loves touch.
Bubbles, each
nudges the other, deforms.

I mean two lovers or that, if air fills water,
it will not buoy but drop
a body.
As if human, water connives.

Four young men fell out of time
in rain-gorged falls. Water
for a year's growth gnashed
lives that had not hardened,
pliant hazel branches.
Four friends did not interpret
but dived into air.
The river refused to carry.

iii
a tight hallway to run
your hands along
till the drummer drops a beat

iv
On a summer's day comes the news:
Earth could explode,
hit by hurtling rock, Jupiter-deflected,

silk scarves pulverized,
trees snapped like bones. Such things,
my grandmother believed,
are less to worry about than
the rising of yeast.
We sit too much in the room.

v
I shall peel the bark, bleach
each episode in rain and sun,
scour the shell.

When hands touch, a germ passes.
On fresh skin, it grows,
a kiss on the cheek a commotion
of fine hairs,
friction of ants mounting a stem.

And friction is heat, but now,
for now, just words.

vi
Too much, or not enough
is not enough
observed. I trade the dark cup
for blind milk-white. And so
are kisses.
Turn your head
to hear a syllable not spoken
that no one can unsay.

vii
Marriage declares two places at the table—
sunshine in leaves through the window.

viii
The last bonbon, the demise
of yes, the fracture
of sound.

JEFFERSON CARTER

Nature Was My Church

Just when you thought it was safe
to idealize again, to abandon yourself
to something pure & unequivocal,
you learned more from the African Lion
Rescue Project. You learned
how the new king hunts down all
the old king's cubs & severs their spines.

Animal, vegetable or mineral? This time
you choose mineral, dumb & deaf
as the Whatever Stone, that souvenir
from Africa your friends' dinner guests
absently finger as they discuss the future
of NPR or the possible correlations
between ethnic cleansing & table talk.

DAVID CHORLTON

In the Steps of the Rain

> *vemos, si es invisible el pájaro,*
> *el color de su canto.*
> —Octavio Paz

Welcome to daylight
disguised as trees, where the tallest
stop growing for the time
it takes to walk past them,
a few feet more
into the tangle of hanging vines
and rising leaves
while oropendola calls drip
between mimosa and ancient almonds
whose roots measure the years
under ground.
                Ants carry their bullet stings
along earth that never dries
past a frog the color of what surrounds him
while a sheet of light falls
through a gap in the canopy
to illuminate a second
in a howler monkey's life
as he swings in silhouette
against a patch of sky melting
into foliage.
            One of all the trees
stands draped with epiphytes but strong
enough to carry everything that grows
upon it. Stoop to enter
and look up. It is taller inside
than out. There are clouds
where it opens into space, and in its empty
core are bats washed in darkness,
holding to textures made by centuries

of rain climbing back to where
it fell from,
           where the Green macaws
send out their morning cries
to clear a space to fly through. The other
birds remain invisible: attila, euphonia,
manakin, each with its signature
notes imprinted on air
in all the colors of its plumage
that glow against
                 the red,
yellow, and black bands of silence
marking the progress of the coral snake.

DAVID CHORLTON

Sky Island Encounters

Once there was a turkey strutting
down the path, and once
a golden snake
stretching long to soak up warmth;
once a deer

stopped suddenly in time
when we were in that moment;
and once a bear
passed along the far edge
of a stream
on his way to the saddle where ferns

make lace of the light.
Once a lizard
turned to amethyst before us
and once the ground

swelled with toads that bubbled
through the dust.
A fox once

leapt out of the moon
and sat on the road.
We saw them all. They did not stay,
but turned for wherever
they needed to go,

as the ocelot did
who lived here
once.

ALLISON DELAUER

The Muriana Poems

    (Two collages in response to the texts of John Muir)

Me, God, the Rock, and Where God Put it.

With him it is all—
And you Satan & Company
Flowing waters will quench the would-be-fires
As well dam for water-tanks the people's cathedrals
Principal—principalities—Hellfires 1906
The roaring of muddied flooded
No holier temple has ever been consecrated by the heart of man

And we drink.

*

History is an accident. How it wrings out one man…
Agency and agency thwarted
The will / the hand.

May 29th, 1870

The earliest azaleas have opened and are ready to burst
We have sunshine every morning from a bright blue
History is an accident

the world though made—is still being made
Epiphany—a sudden

The earliest azaleas have opened and are ready to burst

You seem to understand me better than I do myself
pink, and white vapor cross a startling blue

question the rock

if you would forsake me

even the stones would cry out

I would cry with the stones I would sing
Are you the god in the rock? Steady as rock
Go to the mountain
I burst with a bright blue, I am exactly brim full
you seem to understand me better than I do myself

ALLISON DELAUER

Kaweah River Landscape

Granite walls, and veins of quartz
powdery white waves of weight
freckles of pyrite. Silent.

As a child, I scrambled to the top,
fit my concave belly to convex rock.
The mountain was pregnant with boulders.
My eyeballs filled to the lashes with
stony vistas: weathered igneous,
eroded lime.

The bald Moro poses
between pointed peaks—
He's a craggy metamorphosis
some slow slight of hand summoned these

while the river works
to open hollows, pebbles spin, waltz watery,
carve a womb where the sun traps a pool,
so tiny things breed, die, reek—
taint the water green, taint it black.
Flash floods, spring thaws, wash them
barren again.

Such cycles quicken, loudly,
like bright leaded light, seasoned.
This is when bones grow.

My fingers drew to stone cleavage:
slipping slate, washed limestone to marble.
I tracked the striations with my fingernail—

This time, child's time,
moments collect like gravel.
The rain barrel overflows—
Water rusts the wheelbarrow.

Earth time takes a raucous ride on the back of a glacier,
while our lives to stone time—our moments—pass by, fly by

like how film flickers, whips by, set on the wrong time.

Remember me? Please answer.

Now my palm rests on her beveled corner,
the conglomerate is neck high and speckled with lichen
my toe seeks its foothold, I push up, shift my hips,
my thigh squeezes a flat space

I'm rolling over on top of this stone, eyes closed,
listening.

BILL GLOSE

Kudzu

Emperor of a new continent,
shoots spread like snakes
gliding through a manger.
Each slithering touch of earth
leaves behind knotted crowns
like husks of spent skin.

Sweet flowers blossom into
purple dragons, first hint of
what's to come. Tentacles race
a foot a day while pods lay
dormant, nesting vipers waiting
months and years to strike.

Time creeps. Mountains, valleys,
great plains swaddle in green.
Rubbery vine chews soil, drains
bark. When python flexes
muscle, it blots out sun,
swallows landscapes whole.

LYNN HOFFMAN

River Song

—to be accompanied by banjo

The Asif river tumbles
From the hills down to the plain
He gives a home to hawks and trout
The Asif is his name

Gravity and water play
A million-inning game
We called that game the Asif.
The Asif is its name.

The Asif meets the Ithad,
down where the cedars grow
The cedars stain her water
And strain the melting snow.

The Ithad's quite the lady
She curves, she coos, she smiles
She's a house for bass and heron
As she runs her hundred miles.

The Ithad meets the Asif
In a wood that's filled with game
With their arms around each other
they give birth to the Anayme

We sing songs about the river and
Its gods and lore and fame
We call it Mighty, Swift and Strong
As if It had A name

As if a name could stop it
Or make it toe the line
But the name is a just a lie like
You and Yours and Me and Mine.

Old Adam named the animals
And Eve invented Crime
But the one who laughs at all our names
Is jolly Brother Time.

And everything's a river
And everything is his
We love the things that aren't real
And hate the thing that is.

And we sing songs about the river and
Its gods and lore and fame
We call it Mighty, Swift and Strong
Asif Ithad Aname.

LYNN HOFFMAN

after the ocean left town

last saturday morning at a quarter past two
the tide left town and it stayed
we were mostly glad to be rid of its mess—
we cheered, though a few of us prayed

pressed for years by the weight of brine
protected from the vulgar air
everything once too gross to float
is lying open, dry and bare.

where once was heaving water
is now shell and sticky land
shortly to be wind-dried
then wind-buried in the sand

from the curve we used to call the beach
we look to where the water's flown
at new real estate with ocean view
at retail space we'd die to own

soon, the lawyers and the cops
will lay out borders: metes and bounds
we'll compete with others up the coast
with their own dried up bays and sounds

of course we'll miss our seafood
and children playing in the waves
and perhaps we'll never notice
when new land turns into graves

or maybe there'll be a moment
when the sea takes back the shore
when we cry and wish we'd prayed for less
and not poisoned life for more.

KAREN PAUL HOLMES

Flowers for You, Japan

> —*In Ikebana, full blooms symbolize past;*
> *awakening flowers, present; buds, future.*

for you, I choose
three red tulip buds
to form an infinite triangle

shin, the tallest stem: heaven
   soe looking up: man
      tai below: earth

three green sprigs of spring
add pleasing balance
harmony without symmetry

early flowers & grasses full of grace
sip the *suiban*'s water
nearby, *haru* frogs sing of renewal.

[Written in response to the 2011 earthquake and tsunami.]

JOSEPH HUTCHISON

Auger

The tractor roars. A few of us
flinch at the viewing holes, then
lean in again, touch our noses
to the wire mesh.
                    The big tractor
roars once more; its massive auger
twists, shakes, sinks a few inches,
jams. The engine coughs up black
exhaust...and a red coal flares
in our brains: the earth's too tough!
But no: they flood the hole with water,
and the great screw spins.
                          They'll stab
pylons deep as the glass tower needs
not to fall. The other foundations,
the ones that will crumble, are
inside us: stupas, kivas, parthenons;
Chartres longs to lay aside its ancient
stones.
           The tractor groans; its auger
wounds us. And yet we linger—
floating like baffled ghosts
at the circles of witness.

JOSEPH HUTCHISON

The Gulf

The marine biologist sinks
a blue-gloved hand into the Gulf,
then draws it out, stunned silent
by blackness dripping from his fingers.

*

The columnist and tele-intellectual,
known back in college as Little Georgie,
owl-eyes the moderator and shakes
off the catastrophe. "Accidents happen."
Capitalism's dangerous, he means.
Big rewards demand big risks.
Market wisdom. No pain, no gain.

*

The heron sails low over the grassy marsh,
its legs sleeved up to the knee-joints in crude,
nowhere to land that isn't poison, nowhere
to stand and snap up a clean fish or two.

*

At the edge of the marsh, a half dozen
former fishermen crouch to wipe oil
off the long leaves of grass, in silence;
their Company contracts ban them
from talking to the media. Their pain
has nowhere to land, but keeps on
circling above the beloved waters,
spiraling lower as the weeks go by.

*

Tony Hayward, CEO of BP (two letters
advertised to mean *Beyond Petroleum*),
speaks freely to CNN. "No one," he says,

"wants this thing over more than I do.
I'd like my life back."
                        Later, he climbs
into a limo that whispers him away
to a throbbing helicopter, thence
to an airstrip where the Company jet
stands ready to loft him back to London,
30,000 feet over the lightless Atlantic.
In his mind he's already holding a tumbler
of Ladybank single malt on the rocks.
How many eleven-thousand-dollar-a-day
paychecks can he "earn" before the Board
cuts him loose?
                Hell—the sooner the better!
How sweet to sway under a golden parachute,
age 54, the rest of a life in front of him....

*

Robots on the sandy bottom
saw at the pipe to ready it
for a capping attempt,
but the boil of oil and methane
keeps on thundering up
in diarrheal billows.

A sickening sight, yes—
but far from where we live.

How sad for those living there!

Our thoughts and prayers—etcetera...

*

Decaying fish at the fouled tideline—
more fish than Jesus conjured up
at Bethsaida. A mockery of miracles!
The Gulf's abundance wiped out
so people like me can drive twenty miles
each way to work, gulp bottled water,
keep leftovers cold for days before
finally tossing them out.

The primordial dead power the pictures
that move me to write, the underwater
cameras that make me an impotent witness.
Even the ink in my pen is implicated,
my better angels beached in slick goop
like pelicans, heads cranked back,
eyes frosted over in the wind.
Even the ink in my pen....

*

Day 46.

TV ads tout BP's commitment to clean-up.

News of a stalled rebound: unemployment, 9.7 percent.

Commercials for the new *Infiniti:* air conditioned to mimic bucolic breezes; the dashboard's wood hand-rubbed with silver dust.

The "spill" (a PR term meaning "eruption") stains everything.

Three thousand square miles of the Gulf's surface sheened or slathered, the Gulf winds infused with stench.

A hundred meters down: the plumes like sprawling Rorschachs, petro-globs tumbling like fallen angels toward the Dry Tortugas, toward the lightless Atlantic.

Ocean floor: the very ground of Being a kind of Pompeii, sooted over by rotting animacules, most so holy they've never acquired a name.

*

Day 47.

You expected,
maybe,
an epiphany....

*

The Empire once made Greece its suburb.
Then the Empire made the Wild West its suburb.
Now the Empire's made the whole globe its suburb.

Poetry: enslaved to Rhetoric,
or worse, Linguistics.

Whatever you expected
clearly will not come to pass.
Only the Gulf dying as we speak.

Only blackness dripping from our pens.

*

And yet—hypocrite poet!—here you sit,
casting your bitter lines out into the Gulf.

*

Between the I who sneers and the I who grieves,
between the one who writes and the ones who read,
between the solitary heart and nullity: the Gulf.

Against our own greed we side with the Gulf.
Against our pride, our numbed spirits, against
the gag shame has stuffed in our mouths—
we speak out. To restore the Gulf we speak out,
speak to restore, if we can, our own trashed nature.

In a tense not past, present, or future—we speak.
(We speak, said the poet, in the *possible tense.*)

Though our voices may vacillate, we speak
for the "flow of unforeseeable novelty" that is
the Gulf. Using words estranged by politicos,
corporatists, postmodernists, we speak up
for both the Gulf within and the Gulf without—
speaking, anyway, to make the possible possible.

[Writing in the "possible tense" is a concept put forward by
Breyten Breytenbach in *Intimate Stranger*. The "flow of unforeseeable
novelty" is from Henri Bergson's description of Time in *The Creative
Mind: An Introduction to Metaphysics*.]

LAURA M. KAMINSKI

Educating the Creek

Take Mark Twain's
Life on the Mississippi
down to the winding creek
and read. This creek is wild
and pristine. It changes
its path in small increments:
a foot here, two there,
a fluid property line
that makes all local acreage
stated in values of "more or less."

Read aloud—I want it to know
what to expect when it gets
to the big city: what the Corps
of Engineers has done to the great
Mississippi, how it has been
"leveed" and channeled—
controlled—for predictability
and safety, how catfish reek,
and barges float, and deer
don't come to drink.

LEE KOTTNER

Advice for City People Who Move to the Country

Don't install
that motion-activated sodium light
next to the house.
That small sun
won't scare the deer
from your garden,
or the raccoons
or the occasional bear
from your garbage cans,
and the low crime rate
is why you moved here.
Make do
with reflectors on your mailbox
to mark your driveway.
You'll learn
to find it by instinct,
like a fox returning to her den.

Please don't importune
the township board
for streetlights.
If you want to be seen,
just wear
reflective tape on your jacket
or those sneakers that
spark like fireflies
with each step.
If we walk in the dark here
we carry flashlights
or go by moonlight,
Orion looking over our shoulder,
and there are no sidewalks
anyway.

And when you go out
on a clear, moonless night,

look up.

Once your eyes adapt,
you'll learn
to love the dark
because it isn't.

CAROLYN KREITER-FORONDA

The Bay's Tributaries

It's not perfect living on a cove.
Sometimes it's sullied by runoff.

At low tide it empties to a mudflat.
High noon, the stench runs me indoors

to ponder matters: To spray or not
to spray the azaleas and roses, riddled

by burgeoning lace bugs and beetles.
To fertilize the lawn, weed-patched

after months of downpours. To consider
what the "Been Heres" say: *Ain't the way*

it sposed to be, builders puttin' up
too many of them waterfront homes.

I think about algae blooming close
to shore, about test-tube tumblers

of bedeviled water, and puzzle over what
to do: How to keep herons and ospreys

returning to these tributaries
year after year. Keep seasoned trees

alive with bird-bellow and blare.
Keep ooze and swale from swallowing

the Bay. Keep the drench and splash
wholesome, the wetlands yearning

for a willowy carpet. Keep
hummingbirds belling

their diminutive wings until
the toil of all that flapping

and sipping sugar-rich liquid
swells in the minds

of the "Come Heres" with a sweet,
translucent, pensive truth.

LORI LAMOTHE

American Primitive

A hawk glides in on the music of lawnmowers.

The light's a sieve,
darkness sifts down.

The wingtips of the hawk
brush the grass
and in a single bound its shadow

soars over the ghosts of television sets
haunting identical houses.

The wingspan of the hawk
cuts a path through the air and disappears
behind night's door.

The sky is webbed with echoes—
ancient currents
that cross and recross the silence.

It is a map drawn in an unseen spectrum,
a legend of lucid gestures.

LORI LAMOTHE

Museum of Natural History

The surface of a lake
heals itself of the wound
made by an outboard motor.

Pines repair the silence,
weave air and space into a sky
that birds can fly through.

Even as glaciers drown
the sea is lapping oil off its paws
and snow fills in the blanks

where old names slept.
Earth holds out its apron
to catch the falling rain

but night is wide.
Water pools at the edges
of malls, parking lots.

Puddles teem with dying planets.

LORI LAMOTHE

Cave of the Great Galleries

You would never guess
not from the surface.

Big block letters laid out
in stereo, white glaring on green
as if the farmer who found

rock blowing wind
is still shouting his name.

When you arrive in Cretaceous
sixteen stories down
what surprises you most is not

the way the music of water
seems so much slower than
the dripping of your own faucet,

not the schools of blind fish
threading paths through fear.

What surprises you most
is how the walls keep opening
into rooms never imagined

what was hidden multiplying
like mirrors blooming.

LORI LAMOTHE

White Pines

Branches shaggy with rain,
they dissolve in mist
like small talk fading
at an unremarkable party.

Still, there's something solid
about the way they cling to form—
ancient architecture
that resists forgetting

and weathers even weather,
leaving me with the certainty
that when sunlight
knifes again through gray

I'll find them exactly as they were,
their shapes cloaked in softness.
But I can't help wanting them to be more
than what they are,

to fire beauty into symbol
and forge an idea of all my mad phoenix dreams rising
out of the illusion
that everything endures.

LAURA LEHEW

Apis Mellifera

she hates being an environmental indicator
but she's on the verge of extermination
colony collapse disorder
pesticides, stress, disease—
another great bee

die off

wildfires in the Midwest rage out of control
2012 breaking heat records
hottest year on record since 1895 burning
nest, nectar and pollen and
the seasonal outlook—

drought

she just can't pollinate what isn't there
failing crops corn, apples, blueberries
their risk—16 billion dollars
one out of three bites of food

she knows, she's been there before
the Great Depression, the dust bowl now
the world economy in a Great Recession

collapse

Whatever happened to acid rain?

JAMES B. NICOLA

Damsel Earth

Our blades found her veins
Brave nerves flinched   We shuddered
For the lode was rich

She   depleted by
Our quests for pretty surfaces
Rumbled cleft with scars

Her gold had been taken
Already   And her diamonds.
We saw   but denied

To keep on drilling
Like writers at a blank page
Ravenous for more

Now I too   bottomless
Of blood and inspiration
Mine the gold of fools

SCOTT OWENS

Owned

after a line by W. S. Merwin

On the last day of the world
I want to sit on the ground
beneath any tree I can find,
hopefully one on a hill
with a prospect of sky and water,
whatever color they may be,
and I want to reach my fingers
through blades of grass around me
and down into the earth itself,
still cool and moist as flesh,
and I want to bring a handful
up to my nose and breathe in
the scent of it, and the scent of the air,
and the hint of water in both of them,
and I want to remember that this
is everything we were made from
and everything we made,
and I want to find the one
word that says all of this
and breathe it out
with my last breath as a prayer,
as homage, as celebration.
It will not matter if I am alone.
It will not matter how I am dressed
or whether I am clean and well-sated.
It will not matter whose tree it is.
All will be welcome to join me.
There will not be, nor ever has been
anything proprietary in this
thing we call living at the last.

LEE PATTON

Everlasting Trespass

Slag Pile at the Source

As wilderness, the top of this glacial valley
was pretty hopeless. Stunted spruce,
tortured at timberline, lined a two-track
path into defunct mining camp. Hunkered
under the Great Divide, 1850s shacks
collapsed side by side with 1950s steel
outbuildings. Silver mine, we guessed,
then uranium. Rusted warning signs,
Cold War symbols, dark triangles within
black circle: DANGER. RADIOACTIVE!
The wire fence beaten, ignored. KEEP OUT.

Of course, we let ourselves in, tamping down
the wire with our boots. Sandwiches on a dead
miner's imploding porch. Vista of the whole
valley, subalpine fir giving way to lodgepole
and aspen, woods punctured with orange slag,
mine tailing piles wherever some seeking
soul with a shovel thought to punch a hole.

We spotted a slag pile just down the path.
A snowpatch seeped orange-brown slush,
a trickle spurting who-knew-what, arsenic,
uranium juice? The slag heap fed dead pools,
cascading into toxic stream then coursing
down valley. "The stinkin' source," one of us
knew, "of the South Platte River. The wellspring
of the water we drink down in the city"—
source of the rapids feeding pine canyons,
fresh with everlasting trespass, tainting
the mess we have made.

LEE PATTON

Field Study in Disturbed Soil

The new science teacher stresses "disturbances."
He fingers wispy whiskers meant to disguise
his youth, then cautions the Biology kids and me,
"We may not find a true vestige of native biotics."

Invited to his field trip above our bursting school,
I'm sun-blind in September noon. String squares
mark biosphere samples, disturbances older
than these kids' parents, fields still unhealed.

Toxic invaders took root after we scraped away
our old skin of buffalo grass. A boy strolls up,
twirling string: "Sir, I think I've found it"—He points
past invasive weeds. "There. Oak. Native grasses!"

Each team leaves off stringing the weeds to follow
their teacher to hidden patches of wild. Cool, he hides
his ardor: "Class, notice the mounting size and health
of the grasses and oaks as they amble upslope here."

Surviving scrub oak seeks the ramparts of tract homes,
clipped by mown lawns. Now we find spiders weaving.
Mice dart from chipmunks. Wings sweep and thrust,
warbled songs spin rhythm thicket to thicket.

In thrall of birds' music on the breeze, the kids quiet.
Teams of flax-haired sophomores note first gilded leaves.
I note how the golf green slithers toward the new jail.
Past distant pioneer graveyards, bulldozers bury pasture,

heaving earth for parking lots. When I started teaching here,
deer scored the track, cattle studied the library windows,
and antelope high-jumped where Deer Run Drive sprints
past Antelope Ranch Estates, but I keep that to myself. We're

fated for overpriced boxes dropped into disturbed soil, so
why let the past interlope? The teacher holds up wheaten
stalks, like banners of a doomed flamboyance, their fig-
like leaves cover enough for our expulsion from Eden.

LYNN PEDERSEN

How to Speak Nineteenth Century

Forget about the nomenclature
of the moon: lunar impact craters, rilles; your voice
translated into fiber optics or beamed pinpoint to pinpoint
on the planet. Here, all words are spoken to someone's face.
Earth. Seeds. Thresher. Plow. Timber'd.

So unnerving, you say,
having to look someone that long in the eye, just speaking
your mind. Or too involved, in the first place,
the five-mile walk to your friend's house,
your skirt catching on the field grass.

You need to know not hydrogen, oxygen, H_2O, but
water: where to find it, how to dig
for it, how to ford it, how to keep a well from running dry.

Not chlorophyll and photosynthesis,
the word is *harvest*—the hard "t"
uncompromising as hunger—

sunup and *sundown*, light.
Forget meteorology, you need to know
bird migration, insect hatches, animal hibernation—
what the falling leaves tell you.
When the blossoms of the apple tree fall, plant corn. In short,

the world is still whole to you.
Each molecule. Each syllable. Each grain.

LYNN PEDERSEN

The Rift

Three months now I've been waiting
for your letter. And today, I discover
Madagascar—how it was torn away from Africa
sixty-five million years ago
and the gap
filled with water.
The same thing is happening
in the Great Rift Valley.
You can't see the seam
beneath the grass, but the land imperceptibly
strains north and east,
inching towards the Indian Ocean.

The animals don't know,
or if they know, don't seem to care.
A bird bends its head,
scratches the ground.
Shadows of trees grow longer,
rotate around trunks
like sundials.

And I imagine evolution—how amphibians
used to be fish, grew legs
and lungs—
branched off.

LINWOOD RUMNEY

Low Tide in Penobscot Bay

i.

At low tide, clam diggers
once peppered the mudflats,
punching gloved hands into
soggy clay. With almost
every jab they caught the deeper
briny stench and stony clams.

Now the mudflats are almost empty,
and divers dig in the bay for clams
that could once be summoned
by anyone with the will to make a fist.

ii.

A circus ferry once ran up and down
the coast, from Cape Cod to Bar Harbor—
with an elephant, a tiger, and an osprey
they claimed was an eagle—but the boat
caught fire leaving Searsport
out past Deer Isle. The crew jumped ship first
then the circus performers,
then the animals. The elephant
couldn't take the cold
and the osprey couldn't fly.
As the tide returned, fire consumed the ferry,
and water. Still, some people claim
the tiger made it to the island.

iii.

And now at low tide I walk
along the beach with my wife
as her son pokes through windrows
of seaweed, uncovering crabs
that lift their defiant claws

and skitter toward the water.
We come upon a jellyfish
cast up by surf, dead
but still poisonous—a dark
red, with tentacles folded under,
a ripe and formless gem.

ERIC PAUL SHAFFER

Yadokari: Hermit Crab, Okinawa

He borrows his house, as I borrow mine.
                              We are strangers where we live.

This little crab makes me think
I would crawl around the world with my belongings on my back,
     drag my life behind me every day,
                     to live
in the same world of open sand, empty shells, brilliant blue.

In hand, the hermit crab lives up to the name,
                         a shell closed with claws
but a warm breeze of breath will bring him out.

Set on the shore, he works a way through humps of white sand,
broken branches of coral, sun-bleached beer cans,
                         human footprints.

Life is kind. Move on. Carry what you can.

WALLY SWIST

In the Shade of a Cave

We hike halfway up Mount Toby to where the gorge drops
off and takes the thin stream of Roaring Brook down

toward the culvert beneath train tracks to Cranberry Pond.
I explain that the water is normally roaring every spring

from the snowmelt; however, not having much of a winter
has affected the watersheds. I illustrate that usually

the force of the brook hammers the stones, that the sound
mixes with the ionization of the water rising above the cliffs,

so that you can see, hear, and smell the torrent all at once.
In giving Bob a guided tour of the flora bordering the trail

this mid-April, I find the Quaker Ladies grouped in blue
and white clusters at the bottom, in the scrub meadow that

overlooks the pond. Farther up where I warn him
that here is where the trail begins to become steep, I spot

one nodding purple trillium, then point out the others
blazing their own trail up the slope. He aims the camera

to shoot his photographs of what he describes
as their flowers *looking downward,* and I explain that is why

part of their name includes the word *nodding.* He tells me
how he was an infantryman in the Battle of the Bulge,

one of four soldiers out of a platoon of forty who survived
the surging stormtroopers. I point to the bright yellow

discs of inflorescence of coltsfoot flourishing beside
a trickle of a stream cutting its way through the black mud.

There! I exclaim, and identify the four-lobed lush purple
flowers of hepatica, whose royal hues can be easily missed

due to their diminutive size among leaf litter. I speak
with an intended ebullient clarity that I hope he remembers

when we find the clearing beneath the mossy cliffs halfway
up the mountain, speckled white with the luscious

blossoming of bloodroot. I inform him that there is only
a two-week window of our seeing this perennial in the wild,

of which he shows his rapt appreciation by taking one
photograph after another. *Do you see that one,* I say, placing

one of his hands in one of mine, as I draw a straight line
to where one bloodroot flower grows in the shade of a cave

in the cliffs. *Oh, I see,* he answers, then continues:
Yesterday I couldn't feel my hands and feet from the trench foot I got

in the battle. They only gave us thin gloves, so we could fire our rifles.
My feet froze, since the boots they gave us were not much,

and the socks were too goddamn thin! We look at each other,
with mutual understanding beneath green cliffs, whose

natural architecture we both admire, among blossoms
of bloodroot that star the entire vertical rise in the sunlight.

LILLO WAY

High Winds

Down in the abandoned duck blind, the mallards
  heard the warning and battened themselves.

    There is not so much as a crow in sight
      and there's never not a crow in sight.

        You could almost imagine the eagles had made
          their way back to the endangered species list
          and the herons had decided to go hungry.

            But the gulls were born and bred to these swirling gusts
              and as I stand watch on my third floor balcony,
                a group of seventeen swerve a curve off my right shoulder

              and bank low so I have their backs and the dorsum
                of their wings and they are whiter than doves,
              whiter than angels in their unison turning of thermals.

          If Mark Morris choreographed birds, he'd have made
          this phrase of movement and costumed it stark white
        against a boiling dark backdrop just like this

      and Busby Berkeley, infinite balconies above mine
      would stand up, multiply himself by four dozen
    and give Mark a kaleidoscopic ovation

    and I, no greater than a glass chip wedged
  in a microscopic corner of the turning windscope,
would join him in deafening applause.

LILLO WAY

Death in Big Sur

A log-jam dams-worth of disattached dead-matter.

Vines snake along branches, stake their livelihoods
so tenaciously that when they die they remain right there,
gyring the long branch, feet and toes gripping
years after death, clinging as in life
and hell to remove.

The verdant, the golden, the mind-boggling beautiful
right alongside amputated limbs (arms to the elbow,
legs to the knee) leprosy'd and or just deep-rutted,
washed down riverbeds, ravines and canyons.

In the Pacific Northwest, the dead are covered in moss
and the living too, should they stand still long enough.
In the Southeast, they're enshrouded in kudzu,
in the Northeast, silenced by ice and snow.
But here in Big Sur, the dead are exposed
in grays, in browns, by burl, by burn.

Dead we are,
they seem to be saying,
on the hillside, hilltop,
bend in the creek,
bottom of the landslide,
dwell on us.

LILLO WAY

Foraging

I'm searching for something in the sea arrow grass
and maybe it's not the samphire, cilantro or goosefoot
I've been told grows here in the gravelly wind.

Something's craving sucked me from the fire-warmth
to smack me in the face with salted damp
and send my scraped hands and streaming nose
to search through peppergrass and stinging nettles,
among poisonous pokeweed blooming
near the lords-and-ladies who stuff
vermillion berries into their heavy hoods
while my toes turn the ivory color of corpses.

Partridge berry and blackberry brambles
entangle my slime-sogged ankles—they grip, I pitch
facefirst into the mud and before a sob flies up its wail
and curls into the mist like wild legume vines—
my nostrils gasp the perfume of ramps and rank garlic,
dandelion and borage blossoms, pungent watercress
and vanilla, the underscent of meadowsweet.

Today offers no particular reason for wailing
but the clouds are black on dark on pale,
sap sticks my fingers tight, dirt slap-paints my cheeks,
insects on leaves under leaves have adapted to my legs
and the smells—now wild fennel, now wood sorrel,
now goat's beard, spiderwort and deadly arum—
bind me fast with all foragers, plunderers,
gleaners and thieves, all of us singing out
our earth-engendered, earth-destined howls.

MARTIN WILLITTS, JR.

Communion with the Trees

> *"(trees...) apostles of the living light"* —Wendell Berry

I come for communion
arriving to a place so thick with leaves
and lost light, saplings do not stand
a chance of survival.
What is cut or on fire
separates the living from the dead.
I have come to make my peace,
to find what others avoid.

In this lost light, one could lose themselves.
When that happens
new purpose is found, energy renewed,
all things open up and release.

*

This area is crowded and condensed,
compacted with pines, maples, oak, birch.
It would take a great apocalypse too cleanse it.
It needs a reaping. This is the way of recovery
and new life: the old makes way for the new.

I have come to this place
in search of the sacred and find
what light filters down
is not some common light struggling
to find its way. It nurtures the small, hidden
things, low to the clustered ground.

Something full of sound finds my bones.

*

I came to this untouched forest
to be in silence, to be touched by silence.
I needed to hear what silence said to me.

I did not come for benediction,
or repentance, or seeking forgiveness,
or inner peace. I came for a message.

I came for silence
among silent things, far from noise
and distraction.

Sometimes I leave empty-handed,
like branches with its leaves shook out.
Other times, I am fused with light
and birdsong, fingers having touched ferns
and moss and dampness of silence.
Still other times, I learn one more thing
about the hidden secrets.

*

The apostles were not there
when they were needed.
They hid, scared for their lives,
when it was their soul
they should have been watching.

They did not witness.
They did not believe.
They tore at their skin like it was leaves.

When they were uprooted
they found their way
through a forest
to belief.

*

Sometimes, the forest blesses.

I am not looking for comfort
or companionship. Communion is
a way to talk, not necessarily out loud,
but within. You allow for an exchange,
opening to possibilities.

*

In thousands of Carolina wren songs,
one song is for me.
It is not too late to answer back.
I must say something worth saying.
You have to stand in the present
to let such music in.

DIANA WOODCOCK

Dugong

The problem with marine biologists,
she complains after the lecture
as we walk to the car to drive home
through congested city streets,
is they believe the world revolves
around whatever species they've chosen
for their life work. In the long run,
does it really matter, she asks,
whether or not we save the dugong
and manatee? Won't the world go on
just fine without them?

The secret of marine biologists,
I explain as we sit seemingly forever
in a traffic jam, is they've observed
how the world revolves around another
species till they've been knocked off-center
and are happy now being just one more
kind of organism on the third of nine
planets revolving around an ordinary sun.

Silent sirenian sea cow, content
all these seven and a half thousand years
to graze your flowering sea grasses
in mangrove channels and the lee sides
of inshore islands, you've persevered
as humans hunted you for meat and hides—
stealing even the tears from your eyes.
Do you ask too much now, shy legendary
mermaid, secretive in your sea grass meadows?
Just a few marine protected regions?

Let no more of your tears and semen
be stolen and sold as aphrodisiac.

May you be left alone in your Red Sea,
Arabian Gulf, off Africa's east coast,
Australia's north.
Shall I name you, every one,
Beautiful Mermaid?

DIANA WOODCOCK

Desert Ecology Lesson 19: Angiospermae—Dicotyledoneae

Everything that seems empty is full of the angels of God. —St. Hilary

Best time and place to perceive
the radiance of mind's true nature:
hour preceding dawn in the desert

before day takes precedence,
bringing everything to light.
All seeming at first empty, deserted.

But look closer: the annual polygamous-
monoecious herb, devils thorn, is thriving,
its flowers ripening under the surface.

The delicate thread-stem carpetweed
is donning its green flowers.
In every depression along margins

of cultivated land, in shady moist places,
on dry salines, Her floral presences
stretching your boundaries to the max.

Realizing the fullness of the seemingly empty
desert, holy presences abounding there,
you'll never want to leave, having reached

deep inside where the center holds.
Hour before dawn, words having lost
all meaning, you'll float across the Empty

Quarter like a Mute swan, oblivious to
time, trailing your toes through drifted
sand, heaven under your feet, each

formation—shamal-sculpted—
rising like a jubilant proclamation.
You'll hear an angel applauding

each flower ripening, as your
mind's true radiance shines
bright as the Harvest Moon.

RAY ZIMMERMAN

Water

Look through our disguise.
Find we are water.
Spread us thin and cast
for trout among rogue molecules,
deuterium laced water

Distill us and build a bomb,
aided by that heavy water.
Trap us behind dams
generate power
as we fall homeward.

Use us to polish silver.
Expiate every blemish.
Leave a shine.
Sail hard to leeward
on liquid, once part of a star.

Drink us down
when you finish Pilates.
You too are water,
at least 98 percent, and
not enough to go around.

CONTRIBUTORS

Born in Baghdad, raised in Brooklyn, living in Texas, **Bint Arab** is perpetually out of place and comfortable with that. She is an emerging writer with stories published online at *Toasted Cheese*, *Yellow Mama*, and *Expanded Horizons*; and in print in *Best New Writing 2013*. She administers the bibliophilia.org writers' forum.

Paula Ashley is a retired software engineer. She lives in Arizona with her husband and an abundance of birds that hang out on the solar fountains in their backyard. Paula has had poems published in *Arizona: 100 Years, 100 Poems, 100 Poets*; *Avocet*; *Merge*; *New Fraktur Arts Journal*; *The Blue Guitar Magazine*; *The Examined Life: A Literary Journal of the University of Iowa Carver College of Medicine*; and *Voices on the Wind*. She is the winner of the Best Poem Contest for *OASIS Journal 2013* and has poems in *Four Chambers*.

Shawn Aveningo is a globally published, award-winning poet who can't stand the taste of coconut, eats pistachios daily and loves shoes...especially red ones! (redshoepoet.com). Shawn's poetry has appeared in over 80 literary journals and anthologies, including LA's *PoeticDiversity*, which recently nominated her work for a Pushcart Prize. She's given birth on two continents, and her three children make her an extremely proud "mama bear." She was the founder and host of the popular Verse on the Vine poetry series in Folsom, CA. Since moving to Portland, Oregon in 2014, Shawn has become the new designer of the online *VoiceCatcher Journal*, designs poetry books and anthologies via The Poetry Box® and has recently launched *The Poeming Pigeon: A Literary Journal of Poetry*.

Peggy Aylsworth is a retired psychotherapist living in Santa Monica, CA. Her poetry has appeared in numerous literary journals, including *Beloit Poetry Journal*, *Tampa Review*, *Poetry Salzburg Review*, *Yuan Yang* (Hong Kong), *White Rabbit* (Chile), and is [forthcoming] in *The Wallace Stevens Journal*. Her work also appears in the anthology *Out Of The Depths*.

Mary Jo Balistreri has two full books of poetry, *Joy in the Morning* and *gathering the harvest* by Bellowing Ark Press; and a chapbook, *Best Brothersby*, Tiger's Eye Press. She has recent work in *Parabola*, *The Hurricane Press*, *Plainsongs*, *The Avocet: Journal of Nature Poetry*, *Kentucky Review*, *Crab Creek Review*, *Quill and Parchment*, *Ruminate*, *The Homestead Review*, *The Heron's Nest*, *Acorn*, and *A Hundred Gourds*. Poetrystorehouse has offered videos and a sound scape of two of her poems. She has six Pushcart nominations, and two Best of the Net. She is a founder of Grace River Poets (outreach for women's shelters, churches, and schools). Visit her at maryjobalistreripoet.com.

Ruth Bavetta's poems have been published in *Rattle, Nimrod, Tar River Review, North American Review, Spillway, Hanging Loose, Rhino, Poetry East,* and *Poetry New Zealand,* among others, and are included in the anthologies, *Wait a Minute, I Have to Take off My Bra; Feast; Pirene's Fountain Beverage Anthology; Forgetting Home;* and *Twelve Los Angeles Poets.* She has published two books, *Fugitive Pigments* and *Embers on the Stairs.* A third book, *No Longer at this Address,* is forthcoming. She loves the light on November afternoons, the smell of the ocean, a warm back to curl against in bed. She hates pretense, fundamentalism and sauerkraut.

Delaware native **Nina Bennett** is the author of *Sound Effects* (2013, Broadkill Press Key Poetry Series). Her poetry has appeared in numerous journals and anthologies including *Hartskill Review, Reunion: The Dallas Review, Houseboat, Bryant Literary Review, Yale Journal for Humanities in Medicine, Philadelphia Stories,* and *The Broadkill Review.* Awards include 2014 Northern Liberties Review Poetry Prize, second-place in poetry book category from the Delaware Press Association (2014), and a 2012 Best of the Net nomination.

Nancy Bevilaqua was born in New York City. She worked there from 1988-1998 as a caseworker/counselor for people with AIDS, the homeless, etc. She's also worked as a freelance travel writer, and her articles have appeared in *National Geographic Traveler, Coastal Living, the South Florida Sun-Sentinel,* several in-flight magazines, and other publications. Her poems have been published in or are forthcoming from *Tupelo Quarterly, Juked, Hubbub, Madhat Lit, Atticus Review, Kentucky Review, Menacing Hedge, Construction, Iodine,* and other journals.

A lifelong resident of New York State, **Marion Brown** lives in Yonkers. One of her careers was on Wall Street. Her poems have appeared in *Barrow Street, Big City Lit, DIAGRAM, Kestrel, the Women's Review of Books* and elsewhere. She has reviewed poetry in *Big City Lit* and *Poetry International.* In 2012, her poem "In the Dock, Fagin Reflects" received First Prize in the Portico Library Poetry Competition. Her second chapbook, *The Morning After Summer,* has just been published by Finishing Line Press.

Jefferson Carter has lived since 1953 in Tucson, where, after thirty years, he recently retired as the Writing Department Chair at Pima Community College, Downtown Campus. Currently, he's a passionate volunteer with Sky Island Alliance, a locally based environmental organization.

Alan Catlin has been publishing for five decades in the small, the minuscule, the unknown and the well known, from *Wordsworth's Socks* to *The Literary Review,* and many places in between. His archival collection of small press publications is now part of the University of Buffalo Special Collection. His most recent full-length book of poetry is *Alien Nation,* a compilation of four thematically related chapbooks.

David Chorlton was born in Austria, grew up in Manchester, England, and lived for several years in Vienna before moving to Phoenix in 1978. Arizona's landscapes and wildlife have become increasingly important to him and a significant part of his poetry. In September 2015, he will participate as a poet in the Fires of Change exhibition at the Coconino Center for the Arts in Flagstaff (sponsored by the Southwest Fire Science Consortium, the Landscape Conservation Initiative, and the National Endowment for the Arts).

Carl Chrisman lives with his wife Michelle and son Aidan in Lincoln NE. He has a Master of Arts degree in Counseling Psychology and has led psychotherapeutic writing groups, where clients share their poetry in order to better understand themselves. Besides poetry, his writing interests include prose, flash fiction, and an occasional song. As a student in 1975, he was published by Greg Kuzma in the collection, *Nebraska Poets* (The Best Cellar Press). He and his wife have five children, Travis, Dustin, Kelly, Andrew, Aidan; and five grandchildren, Violet, Charles, Gabriel, Michelle Belle, and Imogene. Carl currently works for a managed health care company in Lincoln.

Joan Colby has published widely in journals such as *Poetry, Atlanta Review, South Dakota Review,* etc. She has received many awards, including two Illinois Arts Council Literary Awards and an Illinois Arts Council Fellowship in Literature. One of her poems is a winner of the 2014 Atlanta Review International Poetry Contest. Formerly editor of *Illinois Racing News,* she lives on a small horse farm in Northern Illinois. She has published 14 books, most recently *Selected Poems,* which received the 2013 FutureCycle Poetry Book Prize; *Properties of Matter* (Aldrich Press/Kelsay Books); *Bittersweet* (Main Street Rag Press); *The Wingback Chair* (FutureCycle Press); *Ah Clio* (Kattywompus Press); and *Pro Forma* (Foothills Publishing). *Ribcage* (Glass Lyre Press) won the 2015 Kithara Book Prize. Colby is also an associate editor of *Kentucky Review* and FutureCycle Press.

Beth Copeland's second poetry collection, *Transcendental Telemarketer* (BlazeVOX books, 2012), was runner up in the North Carolina Poetry Council's 2013 Oscar Arnold Young Award for North Carolina's best book of poetry. Her first book, *Traveling through Glass,* received the 1999 Bright Hill Press Poetry Book Award. Copeland is an Assistant Professor of English at Methodist University. She lives with her husband Phil in a log cabin in rural Scotland County.

James M. Croteau lives in Kalamazoo, MI, with his partner of 30 years, Darryl, and their two Labrador retrievers. He started writing poetry three years ago as a way to cope with growing older, but he then caught the poetry bug. He grew up gay and Catholic in the U.S. south in the '60s and '70s and his writing reflects that experience. His poems have appeared in *HOOT a Postcard review, About Place Journal, Haibun Today, Melancholy Hyperbole, Queer South: LGBTQ Writers on the American South and Assaracus: A Journal of Gay Poetry,* among others. He occasionally blogs about writing at talkingdogsholymen.blogspot.com.

Allison DeLauer's work has appeared or is forthcoming in *Catamaran Literary Reader, Eleven Eleven, Five Fingers Review, Mirage #4/Period(ical), SFStation.com, Squaw Valley Review, burritofile.com,* and *The Throwback.* Her performance collaboration, "All I Wanted to Say," was funded in part by the Zellerbach Family Foundation. This show, as well as her latest collaboration, "Cast Me to Seed/ Umanita," has been translated into Italian and toured in Europe in 2013. She received an MFA from California College of the Arts, residencies from Teatro dei Venti in Modena Italy, Caldera Center for the Arts, and Vermont Studio Center. Since 1996, she has worked with cultural organizations, artists, philanthropists, and social change agents to help them tell their stories. She lives in Oakland, California.

Steven Deutsch was born in Brooklyn in 1946 but spent most of his life in State College, PA where he did research into the fluid mechanics of heart pumps and valves and of drag reduction. He is married with one son who has returned to New York City as a musician.

Anthony DiMatteo's recent poems have been featured in *Avatar Poetry Review, The Cortland Review, Front Porch, Smartish Pace, Tar River Poetry,* and *Waccamaw.* He is the author of *Beautiful Problems: Poems* (David Robert Books) as well as a forthcoming chapbook *Greetings from Elysium* (Finishing Line Press) and a book *In Defense of Puppets* (FutureCycle Press).

Heather Dobbins' poems and poetry reviews have appeared in *Beloit Poetry Review, CutBank, Raleigh Review, The Southern Poetry Anthology* (Tennessee), *The Rumpus,* and *TriQuarterly Review,* among others. She has been awarded scholarships and fellowships to Squaw Valley Community of Writers, Vermont Studio Center, and the Virginia Center for Creative Arts' workshop in Auvillar, France. After several years of earning graduate degrees in California and Vermont, she returned to her hometown of Memphis. Her debut, *In the Low Houses,* was published in 2014. For more information, visit heatherdobbins.com.

Suzanne Dudley-Schon is a life coach and writer who lives in New Hampshire with her husband, many dogs, and a blended passel of five children. She enjoys hiking, being in nature, traveling, and returning home. She is currently at work on a chapbook of poetry as well as a memoir-workbook. In a unique format, she shares her personal and professional insights, both painful and humorous, on the challenging, slow return from becoming her own worst enemy during her supposed salad days. Her work has appeared in *Bloodroot Literary Magazine, GMHA Magazine,* and on her blog: suzannedudley.com.

Bonnie Durrance is a professional photographer and magazine writer by day and poet in the early morning hours. Her mother, a New Yorker for 40 or so years, is 93 and now resides close to Bonnie's home in the Napa Valley. Bonnie views her and those who have crossed the threshold from "mature" to "old" with an increasing passion and desire to understand who they are and who they were, as their bodies recede.

Laura Foley is the author of four poetry collections. *Joy Street* was released in 2014. *The Glass Tree* won the *ForeWord* Book of the Year Award in Poetry (Silver) and was a Finalist for the New Hampshire Writer's Project, Outstanding Book of Poetry. She lives on a woody hill in Vermont with her partner and their three big dogs. laurafoley.net.

Julie Fowler grew up in Pennsylvania, graduated from the University of Delaware with a degree in Business/Philosophy concentration, and recently relocated back to PA from NY. Her work (under the name Julie Stuckey) has appeared or is forthcoming in many literary journals and anthologies, including *A Handful of Dust, Amoskeag, Anderbo, Apropos Literary Journal, Blast Furnace, Broad River Review, Dove Tales Literary Journal, Moonshot Magazine, Open to Interpretation/Intimate Landscape, Prairie Wolf Press Review, Seven Hills Review, This Great Society, Verdad,* and *Wilderness House Literary Review.*

Bill Glose is a former paratrooper, Gulf War veteran, and author of the poetry collections *Half a Man* (FutureCycle Press, 2013) and *The Human Touch* (San Francisco Bay Press, 2007). In 2011, he was named the *Daily Press* Poet Laureate. His poems have appeared in numerous publications, including *Narrative Magazine, Poet Lore,* and *Southern California Review.* Now a full-time writer, he undertakes intriguing pursuits—such as walking across Virginia and participating in a world-record-setting skinny dip event—and writes about them for magazines. His website (BillGlose.com) includes a page of helpful information for writers.

Taylor Graham is a volunteer search-and-rescue dog handler in the Sierra Nevada. Her poems appear widely, including *American Literary Review, The Iowa Review, The New York Quarterly, Poetry International, Southern Humanities Review,* and the anthologies *California Poetry: From the Gold Rush to the Present* (Santa Clara University) and *Villanelles* (Everyman's Library). Her latest book is *What the Wind Says* (Lummox Press, 2013), about her 40 years training, living, and searching with her canine partners. A new collection, *Uplift,* is forthcoming from Cold River Press.

Karen Greenbaum-Maya, retired clinical psychologist, German major, two-time Pushcart nominee and occasional photographer, no longer lives for Art but still thinks about it a lot. Her poems and photos have appeared in *Sow's Ear Poetry Review, Off the Coast, Lilliput Review, Blue Lyra Review, Measure, Conclave, Women's Studies Quarterly, B O D Y,* and *The Centrifugal Eye.* Kattywompus Press published her two chapbooks, *Burrowing Song* (2013) and *Eggs Satori* (2014). She believes that if you want to hit someone with a fish, you should just hit them with a fish, unless you don't have a fish. (See cloudslikemountains.blogspot.com.)

Nancy Gustafson has published poetry, short fiction, and articles in anthologies and journals, including *Time of Singing: a magazine of Christian poetry; Shadow and Light: a Literary Anthology on Memory* (Monadnock Press); *My Kitchen Table: a Gathering Place for Writers* (Sweet Pea Press); *So Long: Short Memoirs of Loss and Remembrance* (Telling Our Stories Press); *Child of My Child* (Gelles-Cole Literary Enterprises); *Angel Face—a rosary-based poetry publication* (MaryAnka Press); and *Beautiful Women: Like You and Me* (Baxter Press).

Lois Marie Harrod's 13th and 14th poetry collections, *Fragments from the Biography of Nemesis* (Cherry Grove Press) and the chapbook *How Marlene Mae Longs for Truth* (Dancing Girl Press), appeared in 2013. *The Only Is* won the 2012 Tennessee Chapbook Contest (Poems & Plays), and *Brief Term*, a collection of poems about teachers and teaching was published by Black Buzzard Press, 2011. *Cosmogony* won the 2010 Hazel Lipa Chapbook (Iowa State). She is widely published in literary journals and online ezines from *American Poetry Review* to *Zone 3*. She teaches Creative Writing at The College of New Jersey. Read her work on loismarieharrod.org.

Poet **M. Ayodele Heath** is a graduate of the MFA program at New England College. Heath's honors include a 2009 Dorothy Rosenberg Prize and a McEver Visiting Chair in Writing at Georgia Tech. He has been awarded fellowships from Cave Canem, Summer Poetry at Idyllwild, and the Caversham Centre for Writers & Artists in South Africa and received a grant in Literary Arts from the Atlanta Bureau for Cultural Affairs. His work has appeared in *Crab Orchard Review, diode, Mississippi Review*, as well as featured in anthologies including *Poetry Slam: the Competitive Art of Performance Poetry* (2000), *My South: a People, a Place, a World All Its Own* (2005), and *Southern Poetry Anthology, Volume V, Georgia* (2013). An Atlanta native, he resides online at ayospeaks.com.

Lynn Hoffman has been a merchant seaman, teacher, chef and cab driver. He has published two novels, *The Bachelor's Cat* and *Paula Sherman and the National Rifle Association*. He has also written *The New Short Course in Wine* and *The Short Course in Beer* and *Short Course in Rum*. More than 150 of his poems have been published, and his latest book, *Radiation Days*, is a cancer comedy. Lynn's main influences are Geoffrey Chaucer, William Blake, Billy Collins, Groucho Marx, and Ogden Nash.

Janis Butler Holm lives in Athens, Ohio, where she has served as Associate Editor for *Wide Angle*, the film journal. Her prose, poems, and performance pieces have appeared in small-press, national, and international magazines. Her plays have been produced in the U.S., Canada, and England.

Karen Paul Holmes has a full-length poetry collection, *Untying the Knot* (Aldrich Press, June 2014), and her poems have appeared in publications such as *Atlanta Review, POEM, The Sow's Ear Poetry Review, Kentucky Review, American Society: What Poets See* (FutureCycle Press), and *The Southern Poetry Anthology Vol 5: Georgia* (Texas Review Press).

Paul Hostovsky's latest book of poetry is *The Bad Guys* (2015 FutureCycle Press). His poems have won a Pushcart Prize and two Best of the Net awards. He has been featured on *Poetry Daily, Verse Daily, The Writer's Almanac*, and he was a Featured Poet on the Georgia Poetry Circuit 2013. He makes his living in Boston as a sign language interpreter and Braille instructor. To read more of his work, visit him at paulhostovsky.com.

Ann Howells's poetry appears in *Borderlands, Concho River Review, Crannog* (Ire), *Plainsongs, RiverSedge, Rockhurst Review, San Pedro River Review*, and *Spillway* among others. She serves on the board of Dallas Poets Community, 501c3 non-profit, and has edited *Illya's Honey* since 1999, recently going digital (IllyasHoney.com). She also serves on advisory boards and panels for various other literary organizations, has placed in several national competitions, and frequently serves as judge in poetry competitions. Her chapbooks are *Black Crow in Flight* (Main Street Rag Publishing, 2007) and *The Rosebud Diaries* (Willet Press, 2012). She has been read on NPR, interviewed on *Writers Around Annapolis* television, and been four times nominated for a Pushcart, twice in 2014.

A. J. Huffman has published eleven solo chapbooks and one joint chapbook through various small presses. Her new poetry collection, *Another Blood Jet*, is now available from Eldritch Press. She has three more poetry collections forthcoming: *A Few Bullets Short of Home* from mgv2>publishing, *Degeneration* from Pink Girl Ink, and *A Bizarre Burning of Bees* from Transcendent Zero Press. She is a Multiple Pushcart Prize nominee and has published over 2,100 poems in various national and international journals, including *Labletter, The James Dickey Review, Bone Orchard, EgoPHobia*, and *Kritya*. She is also the founding editor of Kind of a Hurricane Press. kindofahurricanepress.com

Joseph Hutchison is the author of 15 collections of poems, including *Marked Men, Thread of the Real, The Earth-Boat*, and *Bed of Coals* (winner of the Colorado Poetry Award and recently reprinted by FutureCycle Press). He has also co-edited the FutureCycle Press Good Works anthology *Malala: Poems for Malala Yousafzai* and *A Song for Occupations: Poems about the American Way of Work* (Wayland Press). His poetry, short fiction, literary essays, and book reviews have appeared in more than 100 journals in the U.S., Canada, Australia, New Zealand, England, Wales, and Austria. His newest collection, *The Satire Lounge*, and his translation of *Ephemeral*, flash fictions by Mexican writer Miguel Lupián, will appear in Spring 2015 from Folded Word. In September 2014, Hutchison was appointed to a four-year term as Poet Laureate of Colorado. He lives in the mountains southwest of Denver with his wife, Iyengar yoga instructor Melody Madonna.

Laura M. Kaminski grew up in Nigeria, went to school in New Orleans, and currently lives on Carver Creek in rural Missouri. She is the author of *Returning to Awe* and *last penny the sun* (both Balkan Press, 2014); *And Yes, I Dance*, and *Answering the Cuttlefish*. Recent poems have appeared in *The Lake, Kentucky Review, Pilgrimage, Ember: A Journal of Luminous Things, Synchronized Chaos, The Camel Saloon*, and elsewhere. She is an Associate Editor at *Right Hand Pointing*.

Robert S. King, a native Georgian, now lives in Lexington, Kentucky. His poems have appeared in hundreds of magazines, including *California Quarterly, Chariton Review, Hollins Critic, Kenyon Review, Atlanta Review, Main Street Rag, Midwest Quarterly, Negative Capability, Southern Poetry Review,* and *Spoon River Poetry Review*. He has published eight collections of poetry, most recently *Diary of the Last Person on Earth* (Sybaritic Press, 2014) and *Developing a Photograph of God* (Glass Lyre Press, 2014). Robert's work has been nominated several times for the Pushcart Prize and the Best of Net award. He is editor-in-chief of *Kentucky Review*, kentuckyreview.org.

Lidia Kosk is the author of eleven books of poetry and short stories, including two bilingual volumes, *niedosyt/reshapings* and *Słodka woda, słona woda/Sweet Water, Salt Water* (translated into English by Danuta E. Kosk-Kosicka). She has been published in literary journals and anthologies, including *International Poetry Review, Interpoezia, Lalitamba,* and *Notre Dame Review*, in the USA, Poland, Russia, and Japan. She has edited two anthologies. Her poems have been translated into ten languages and into choral compositions and multimedia video presentations. A lawyer, humanitarian, and world traveler, she resides in Warsaw, Poland, where she leads literary workshops and a Poets' Theater.

Danuta E. Kosk-Kosicka is the author of two books: *Face Half-Illuminated,* a book of poems, translations, and prose (Apprentice House, 2014); and *Oblige the Light,* winner of the fifth annual Harriss Poetry Prize (CityLit, 2015). She is the translator for two books by Lidia Kosk: *niedosyt/reshapings* and *Słodka woda, słona woda/Sweet Water, Salt Water*. Her poems, translations, essays, and interviews have appeared in the USA and throughout Europe. She is co-editor of *Loch Raven Review* and a founding member of the DC-ALT association of literary translators. A biochemist by training, she is also a photographer whose work has been exhibited in individual and group shows and used for book covers. She grew up in Poland and lives in Maryland.

Lee Kottner is a writer, educator, union activist, and book artist living in Harlem, NY. Her poetry has appeared in several journals and anthologies and in a chapbook from Blue Stone Press. *Stories from the Ruins,* a hand-bound, hardcover artist's chapbook of 16 poems about the events of 9/11, is in the permanent collections of the Detroit Institute of Arts and MoMA. She's currently working on her next poetry collection and a novel while teaching at CUNY's York College and New York City College of Technology and New Jersey City University.

Carolyn Kreiter-Foronda served as Poet Laureate of the Commonwealth of Virginia from 2006-2008. She holds a B.A. from the University of Mary Washington and M.Ed., M.A. and Ph.D degrees from George Mason University, where she received the university's first doctorate and an Outstanding Academic Achievement and Service Award. In 2007 both universities gave her the Alumna of the Year Award. She has co-edited three anthologies and published seven books of poetry, including *The Embrace: Diego Rivera and Frida Kahlo*, winner of the 2014 Art in Literature: Mary Lynn Kotz Award. Her poems have been nominated for six Pushcart Prizes and appear in numerous magazines, including *Nimrod, Prairie Schooner, Mid-American Review, Best of Literary Journals, Poet Lore* and *An Endless Skyway*, an anthology of poems by U.S. State Poets Laureate. An accomplished visual artist, she teaches art-inspired poetry workshops for the Virginia Museum of Fine Arts.

Judy Kronenfeld's most recent poetry books are *Shimmer* (WordTech Editions, 2012) and the second edition of *Light Lowering in Diminished Sevenths* (Antrim House, 2012), winner of the 2007 Litchfield Review Poetry Book Prize. Her poems have appeared in many print and online journals such as *Calyx, Cimarron Review, The American Poetry Journal, Natural Bridge, Poetry International, Sequestrum, Spoon River Poetry Review, Valparaiso Poetry Review, Women's Review of Books,* and *The Pedestal,* as well as in eighteen anthologies including *Beyond Forgetting: Poetry and Prose about Alzheimer's Disease* (Kent State, 2009), *Love over 60: An Anthology of Women's Poems* (Mayapple, 2010), and *Before There Is Nowhere to Stand: Palestine/Israel: Poets Respond to the Struggle* (Lost Horse, 2012). Her occasional stories and essays have appeared in *Literary Mama* and *Under the Sun,* among other journals. She is Lecturer Emerita, Creative Writing Dept., UC Riverside, and Associate Editor of the online poctry journal, *Poemeleon.*

Lori Lamothe is the author of two full-length poetry collections, *Trace Elements* (Aldrich Press) and *Happily* (Aldrich Press, forthcoming 2015). She has also published several chapbooks, including *Ouija in Suburbia* (Dancing Girl Press). Her poems have appeared or are forthcoming in *Alaska Quarterly Review, Blackbird, Painted Bride Quarterly, The Literary Review, Verse Daily,* and other venues. She lives in New England with her daughter and a red Siberian husky born on Halloween.

Laura LeHew's collections include *Willingly Would I Burn* (MoonPath Press), *It's Always Night, It Always Rains* (Winterhawk Press), and *Beauty* (Tiger's Eye Press). She has poems in *American Society: What Poet's See, Eleven Eleven, Ghost Town, Of/With, PANK* and *Slice.* Laura is on the steering committee for the Lane Literary Guild, volunteers for the Oregon Poetry Association. She interned for, and is a former board member of, CALYX Press. In her other life Laura owns a computer forensics and network security consulting company. She received her MFA from the California College of Arts and edits her small press Uttered Chaos (utteredchaos.org). Forthcoming projects: *Command Line Kung-Fu,* Paul Asadoorian, Tim Medin, Hal Pomeranz and Ed Skoudis; *Mrs.*

Schrödinger's Breast, Quinton Hallett; and books/chapbooks by Roy R. Seitz, Anita Sullivan, and A. Molotkov. She knows nothing of gardens or gardening but is well versed in the cultivation of cats.

Cynthia Linville, a 2012 Pushcart nominee, has taught writing in the English Department at California State University, Sacramento since 2000 and has served as Managing Editor of *Convergence: an online journal of poetry and art* since 2008. Her work has appeared in many publications and several anthologies, and her two poetry collections, *The Lost Thing* (2012) and *Out of Reach* (2014), are available from Cold River Press. Also a photographer and performer, Linville occasionally appears with musicians, including Victor Krummencher of Camper Van Beethoven and Cracker. She invented a poetic form dubbed the Linvillanelle which is profiled on SacPoetryNow.com.

Linda Lowe received her M.F.A. from the University of California, Irvine. A chapbook of her poems, *Karmic Negotiations,* was published by Sarasota Theatre Press, and several of her short plays have been informally staged in Hollywood. Online, her stories have appeared in *The Pedestal Magazine, Right Hand Pointing, The Linnet's Wings, Defenestration Magazine, Gone Lawn,* and others.

Stephanie Madan writes for the print magazine *My Table.* Her column received a 2014 Lone Star Award. She also has poetry published in Texas Poetry Calendar 2015. Her prose has been featured in online magazines and in anthologies such as *Beyond the Nightlight* and *Puppy Love.* Stephanie shares her life with her husband and two white dogs—a qualified white—they are tomboys and have been referred to as walking trash cans with animated tails.

Sage Graduate Fellow at Cornell University (MFA) and Professor of English and Creative Writing at Lock Haven University, **Marjorie Maddox** has published nine collections of poetry—most recently *Local News from Someplace Else; Weeknights at the Cathedral; Transplant, Transport, Transubstantiation* (2004 Yellowglen Prize); and *Perpendicular As I* (Sandstone Book Award)—and over 450 stories, poems, and essays in journals and anthologies. Co-editor of *Common Wealth: Contemporary Poets on Pennsylvania,* she also has eight children's books, including *A Crossing of Zebras: Animal Packs in Poetry* and *Rules of the Game: Baseball Poems.* Her numerous honors include Cornell's Chasen Award, the 2000 Paumanok Poetry Award, the *Seattle Review*'s Bentley Prize for Poetry, an Academy of American Poets Prize, a Bread Loaf Scholarship, Pushcart Prize nominations in both fiction and poetry, and LHU's Honors Professor of the Year. For more information, see marjoriemaddox.com.

J. H. Martin is from London, England but has no fixed abode. His prose and poetry have appeared in a number of places in Asia, Australia, the UK and the USA. For more information, please visit either, thebamboosea.wordpress.com or acoatforamonkey.wordpress.com.

Catherine McGuire has worked with homeless and has also witnessed the destruction of the environment in her almost 60 years on this planet. Her poems have appeared in venues such as: *Avocet, FutureCycle, Green Fuse, New Verse News, Nibble, Portland Lights Anthology* and *Tapjoe*. Her chapbook, *Palimpsests*, was published by Uttered Chaos in 2011, and she has three self-published chapbooks. Her website is cathymcguire.com.

John McKernan grew up in Omaha, Nebraska and is now a retired comma herder/phonics coach after teaching 41 years at Marshall University. He lives—mostly—in West Virginia where he edits ABZ Press. He has published poems in many places from *The Atlantic Monthly* to *Zuzu's Petals*. His latest book is *Resurrection of the Dust*.

James B. Nicola is a New York author originally from Worcester, Massachusetts. *Manhattan Plaza* is his first collection of poetry. He has been widely published in periodicals including *FutureCycle*, the *Southwest, Atlanta* and *Texas Reviews, Tar River, Lyric, Nimrod,* and *Blue Unicorn* stateside, and overseas in *The Istanbul Review* and *Poetry Salzburg*. James won the Dana Literary Award, a People's Choice award (from *Storyteller*) and a *Willow Review* award; was nominated twice for a Pushcart Prize and once for a Rhysling Award; and was featured poet at *New Formalist*. A Yale grad and stage director by profession, his book *Playing the Audience* won a *Choice* award. Also a composer, lyricist, and playwright, his children's musical *Chimes: A Christmas Vaudeville* premiered in Fairbanks, Alaska, where Santa Claus was in attendance on opening night. More at sites.google.com/site/jamesbnicola.

Originally from Greenwood, SC, **Scott Owens** holds degrees from Ohio University, UNC Charlotte, and UNC Greensboro. He currently lives in Hickory, NC, where he recently left his teaching position at Catawba Valley Community College and became the proprietor of Taste Full Beans coffee shop. There he also hosts a monthly reading series, Poetry Hickory. Scott edits *Wild Goose Poetry Review* and serves as vice-president of the NC Poetry Society. His 11th book of poetry, *Eye of the Beholder*, was recently released by Main Street Rag. His work has received awards from the Academy of American Poets, the Pushcart Prize Anthology, the Next Generation/Indie Lit Awards, the NC Writers Network, the NC Poetry Society, and the Poetry Society of SC.

Lee Patton has published work in *The Threepenny Review, The Massachusetts Review, The California Quarterly,* and *Hawaii-Pacific Review*. Other credits include several anthologies, such as *Hawaii-Pacific Review's Best of Decade,* the *Poets On:* series, *XY-Files,* and *Hunger Enough*. New poems appear in *Ellipsis, Memoir Journal,* and *Poetry Quarterly*. Lee's second novel, *Love and Genetic Weaponry: The Beginner's Guide,* appeared in 2009, and a collection of stories, *Au Bon Pain,* came out in May 2012. Awards and activities include the 2006 Short Fiction Award from Colorado Author's League; finalist for the 2001 Lambda Awards for best novel (*Nothing Gold Can Stay*); The Borderlands Playwrights Prize (*The Houseguest*); and the Ashland New Playwrights (*Orwell in Orlando*). New fiction appears in *Adirondack Review* and *Best New Writing 2012*.

Lynn Pedersen's poems, essays, and reviews have appeared in *New England Review, Ecotone, Poet Lore, Southern Poetry Review, Palo Alto Review,* and *Heron Tree.* She is the author of two chapbooks, *Theories of Rain* (Main Street Rag) and *Tiktaalik, Adieu* (Finishing Line Press). Her full-length collection, *The Nomenclature of Small Things,* is forthcoming from Carnegie Mellon University Press in 2016. A graduate of the Vermont College of Fine Arts, she lives in Atlanta, Georgia. Her website is lynnpedersen.wordpress.com.

Richard King Perkins II is a state-sponsored advocate for residents in long-term care facilities. He lives in Crystal Lake, IL with his wife, Vickie and daughter, Sage. He is a three-time Pushcart nominee and a Best of the Net nominee whose work has appeared in more than a thousand publications. In a six-year period, his poems have appeared in *The Louisiana Review, Bluestem, Emrys Journal, Sierra Nevada Review, Roanoke Review, The Red Cedar Review* and *Crannog*. He has poems forthcoming in *The William and Mary Review, Sugar House Review, Old Red Kimono* and *Milkfist*. He was a recent finalist in The Rash Awards, Sharkpack Alchemy, Writer's Digest and Bacopa Literary Review poetry contests.

Connie Post served as the first Poet Laureate of Livermore, California from 2005–2009. Her work has appeared in *The Big Muddy, Calyx, Cold Mountain Review, Crab Creek Review, Comstock Review, The Pedestal Magazine, Slipstream, Spoon River Poetry Review* and *The Valparaiso Poetry Review*. She was the winner of the Cover Prize for the Spring 2009 issue of *The Dirty Napkin* and the winner of the 2009 Caesura Poetry Awards. Her work has received praise from Al Young, Ursula LeGuin and Ellen Bass. She has been short listed for the Muriel Craft Bailey awards (*Comstock Review*) Lois Cranston Memorial Awards (*Calyx*), *Blood Root Literary Magazine* and the Gary Gildner Award (*I 70 Review*). Her first full-length book, *Floodwater* (Glass Lyre Press, 2014) won the Lyrebird award.

Jean Queneau has lived in Golden, CO for over 40 years. She is a graduate of the Univ. of Minnesota with a BA in English. She has taken classes at Univ. of CO Denver as well as with the Foothills Art Center and Rocky Mountain Writers Guild. Jean worked as editor/proofreader at Hazen Research in Golden for nine years and now works part-time in the same role, as well as that of secretary/treasurer for P.B.Queneau & Associates Inc. She is the mother of three, grandmother of four, and a member of Posted Poets.

Mary Ricketson, Murphy NC, has been writing poetry for 20 years, inspired by nature and her work as a mental health counselor. Her poetry has been published in *Wild Goose Poetry Review, FutureCycle Press, Journal of Kentucky Studies, Lights in the Mountains, Echoes Across the Blue Ridge, Freeing Jonah,* and *Red Fox Run.* Her chapbook is *I Hear the River Call my Name,* and a full-length collection of poetry, *Hanging Dog Creek.* She won the gold medal for poetry in the 2011 Cherokee County Senior Games/Silver Arts and silver medal for 2012 and 2013, and first place in the 2011 Joyce Kilmer Memorial Forest 75th anniversary national poetry contest. She writes a monthly column, "Women to Women," for *The Cherokee Scout* and is an organic blueberry farmer.

Kristin Roedell is a retired attorney living in Lakewood Washington. Her work has appeared in over 50 journals and anthologies, including *Switched on Gutenberg, Damselfly, Crab Creek Review,* and the *Journal of the American Medical Association.* She is the author of *Girls with Gardenias* (Flutter Press). She has been twice nominated for Best of the Web and once for the Pushcart Prize. She was the 2013 winner of NISA's 11th Annual Brainstorm Poetry Contest and a finalist in the 2013 Crab Creek Review poetry contest. Her full-length ms., *Down River,* was a finalist in the Quercus Review Press poetry prize and is forthcoming from Aldrich Press. Her website: cicadas-sing.ucoz.com.

Linwood Rumney's poems, nonfiction essays, and translations have appeared in *North American Review, Kenyon Review, Ploughshares, Painted Bride Quarterly, Adirondack Review,* and elsewhere. He's received awards from the St. Botolph Club and the Writers Room of Boston. An editorial assistant for Black Lawrence Press, he lives in Cincinnati, where he is pursuing a PhD as a Taft Fellow.

Sarah Russell's poetry is forthcoming or has appeared in *Red River Review, Misfit Magazine, The Houseboat, Bijou Poetry Review* and *Poppy Road Review,* among others. She is the poetry editor for *Voices* and co-edits *Pastiche,* a local literary journal. Follow her work at SarahRussellPoetry.com.

Paul Saluk lives with his wife Beryl in South Florida. He has published poems in regional and State publications and anthologies. His work has also appeared in Outrider Press editor Whitney Scott's *Seasons of Change—2010* and *A Bird in the Hand—Risk and Flight.* He was a Finalist in the 2010 and 2011 William Faulkner-William Wisdom Creative Writing Contest.

Eric Paul Shaffer is author of five books of poetry, including *Lāhaina Noon; Living at the Monastery, Working in the Kitchen;* and *Portable Planet.* More than 400 of his poems have appeared in more than 250 local and national reviews as well as many in Australia, Canada, England, Ireland, Japan, New Zealand, Scotland, and Wales. Shaffer has received a number of local literary awards, including the 2002 Elliot Cades Award, a 2006 Ka Palapala Po'okela Book Award for *Lāhaina Noon,* and the 2009 James M. Vaughan Award for Poetry. He teaches composition, literature, and creative writing at Honolulu Community College.

Lucille Gang Shulklapper's poetry and fiction appear in many anthologies as well as in five poetry chapbooks including the forthcoming chapbook titled Gloss. Her first picture book, *Stuck In Bed Fred,* has been recently published. At various times, she has led poetry workshops for the Florida Center for the book and those facilitated through the Palm Beach Poetry Festival, taught reading K-college, made recordings for the blind, and raised a family.

Judith Skillman's new collection is *House of Burnt Offerings* from Pleasure Boat Studio. Her work has appeared in *Tampa Review, Prairie Schooner, FIELD, The Iowa Review, Poetry, The Southern Review, Midwest Quarterly Review, New*

Poets of the American West, and other journals and anthologies. Skillman is the recipient of grants from the Academy of American Poets, Washington State Arts Commission, The Centrum Foundation, and other organizations. She taught in the field of humanities for 25 years and has collaboratively translated poems from Italian, Portuguese, and French.

Canadian fiction writer, poet, and playwright **J. J. Steinfeld** is the author of fifteen books, including *Disturbing Identities* (stories, Ekstasis Editions), *Should the Word Hell Be Capitalized?* (stories, Gaspereau Press), *Anton Chekhov Was Never in Charlottetown* (stories, Gaspereau Press), *Would You Hide Me?* (stories, Gaspereau Press), *An Affection for Precipices* (poetry, Serengeti Press), *Misshapenness* (poetry, Ekstasis Editions), *A Glass Shard and Memory* (stories, Recliner Books), and *Identity Dreams and Memory Sounds* (poetry, Ekstasis Editions). His short stories and poems have appeared in numerous anthologies and periodicals internationally, and over forty of his one-act plays and a handful of full-length plays have been performed in Canada and the United States.

Since retiring from a professorship at Marietta College, **Carol Steinhagen** finds herself writing about aging quite often. Typically, she writes about other people's aging but probably takes their experiences personally. She has published most recently in *Rockhurst Review* and *Perfume River Review*, with work forthcoming in *The Comstock Review*, *Third Wednesday*, and *Exit 13*.

Professor of English Emerita, Montclair State University, **Carole Stone**'s most recent poetry collections are *American Rhapsody* (CavanKerry Press, 2012) and *Hurt, the Shadow* (Dos Madres Press, 2013). *Late* is forthcoming from Turning Point. Her most recent poems have been published in *Cavewall*, *Bellevue Literary Review* and *Blue Fifth Review*. She divides her time between East Hampton, NY and Verona, NJ.

Meryl Stratford won the 2013 YellowJacket Press competition for her chapbook, *The Magician's Daughter*. Her poems have appeared in *Rattle*, *Amsterdam Quarterly*, *Comstock Review*, and *The Journal of the Society of Classical Poets*, and have been anthologized in *Crossing Lines*, *Malala: Poems for Malala Yousafzai* and *The Liberal Media Made Me Do It: Poetic Responses to NPR & PBS Stories*. Meryl lives with her husband, Richard Magesis, in Hallandale Beach, Florida.

Wally Swist's books include *Huang Po and the Dimensions of Love* (Southern Illinois University Press, 2012); *The Daodejing: An Interpretation*, with David Breeden and Steven Schroeder (Lamar University Press, 2015); *Invocation* (Lamar University Press, 2015); and *Things I Know I Love: Odes to Food* (Finishing Line Press, 2015). Some of his new poems appear in *carte blanche* (Canada), *Commonweal*, *The Galway Review* (Ireland), *The Linnet's Wings* (Ireland), *North American Review*, and *Pulp Literature* (Canada). Garrison Keillor recently read one his poems on the daily radio program *The Writer's Almanac*.

Laurence W. Thomas has published books of poetry, fiction, humor, and creative nonfiction. His work has appeared in many journals such as *Blue Unicorn, The Antioch Review, Third Coast,* and many others. Thomas is founder and editor of *Third Wednesday,* a literary arts journal.

Sara Toruño-Conley teaches English at Los Medanos College and lives in San Francisco. She received her MFA in Creative Writing from the University of California, Riverside and grew up in the high desert of southern California. Her poems have appeared in the following publications: *Forge, Contraposition, The Café Review, Found: Fiction and Poetry Anthology, Modoc Independent News* (April 2009's Surprise Valley Poetry winner), *The Common Line Project* (honorable mention), *Eclectica, Ginosko, Temenos,* and *Monday Night.*

Sherre Vernon lives, works and writes in Los Angeles, California. Her poetry has been published in over a dozen literary journals, including *Ars Medica, The Coe Review, Fickle Muses, Eclipse* and *The Pedestal Magazine. Green Ink Wings,* her postmodern novella, won the 2005 chapbook award from Elixir Press. In 2008, *The Name is Perilous,* a poetry chapbook, appeared in the final publication of the journal *Ruah.*

Lillo Way's poems have appeared or are forthcoming in *Poet Lore, the Madison Review, Sow's Ear Poetry Review, Poetry East, Third Wednesday, Common Ground Review, Permafrost, Cordite Review* (Australia), *the Bear Deluxe, Tampa Review, Still Point Arts Quarterly, Avalon Literary Review, Northern New England Review, Yemassee, Freshwater, Quiddity, Santa Fe Literary Review, Darkling SLAB* and *WomanArtsQuarterly,* among others. She lives in Seattle.

Richard Widerkehr won two Hopwood Awards for poetry at the University of Michigan and received his M.A. from Columbia University, which he attended on a Woodrow Wilson Fellowship. Two book-length collections of his poems were published in 2011: *The Way Home* (Plain View Press) and *Her Story of Fire* (Egress Studio Press). Tarragon Books published his novel, *Sedimental Journey,* about a geologist. Recent work has appeared in *Rattle, Floating Bridge Review, Northwind Anthology, Poetry Super Highway* and *Crack the Spine.* Poems are forthcoming in *Nomad's Choir, Clay Bird Review, Soundings,* and *Penumbra.*

Martin Willitts, Jr. is a Quaker and organic gardener. He won the International Dylan Thomas Poetry Award. He has poems in *Kentucky Review, Blue Fifth Review, Turtle Island Quarterly, Centrifugal Eye, Stone Canoe, Comstock Review, Poppy Road Review, Nine Mile Magazine,* and others. He has six full-length collections, including national ecological contest winner *Searching for What Is Not There* (Hiraeth Press, 2013); and 28 chapbooks, including contest winner *William Blake, Not Blessed Angel but Restless Man* (Red Ochre Press, 2014). His forthcoming collections include *How to Be Silent* (FutureCycle Press) and *God Is Not Amused With What You Are Doing In Her Name* (Aldrich Press).

Diana Woodcock's first full-length collection, *Swaying on the Elephant's Shoulders*, won the 2010 Vernice Quebodeaux International Poetry Prize for Women. Her chapbooks include *Desert Ecology: Lessons and Visions*, *Tamed by the Desert*, *In the Shade of the Sidra Tree*, *Mandala*, and *Travels of a Gwai Lo*. Widely published in literary journals, her poems have been nominated for the Pushcart Prize and Best of the Net Award. Her second full-length collection, *Under the Spell of a Persian Nightingale*, is forthcoming from WordTech Communications. Her sixth chapbook, *Beggar in the Everglades*, is forthcoming from Finishing Line Press. She has been teaching composition and creative writing courses for eleven years in Qatar at Virginia Commonwealth University's branch campus.

Abigail Wyatt lives near Redruth in the shadow of Carne Brea in Cornwall. Formerly a teacher, she now writes poetry and short fiction, much of which she has been fortune enough to place in a diverse range of magazines and journals. She is the author of two poetry collections and *Old Soldiers, Old Bones and Other Stories*. One of the editors of *Poetry24* and co-editor of the "Murder of Krows" anthologies, Abigail is currently working on a collection of poems arising out of old photographs.

James K. Zimmerman, a Pushcart Prize nominee, is the winner of the Daniel Varoujan Award from the New England Poetry Society, the Hart Crane Memorial Poetry Award, and the Cloudbank Poetry Prize. His work appears in *The Evansville Review*, *Confrontation*, *Atlanta Review*, *Nimrod*, *Passager*, *The MacGuffin*, and *Vallum*, among others. His chapbook, *Little Miracles*, is forthcoming from Passager Press.

Ray Zimmerman is the Executive Editor of *Southern Light: Twelve Contemporary Southern Poets* and author of the chapbook *First Days*. His nonfiction and poetry have appeared in numerous publications. His poem "Glen Falls Trail" appeared in the *Southern Poetry Anthology: Volume VI, Tennessee*, after receiving an award from the Tennessee Writers Alliance.

ACKNOWLEDGMENTS

Many of the works herein, sometimes in earlier versions, appeared previously in other publications and are reprinted with the authors' permission:

Paula Ashley
"Sunset Vista" (*The Blue Guitar*)

Mary Jo Balistreri
"Lady of the Rising Steam" (from the author's book, *gathering the harvest*, Bellowing Ark Press)

Nina Bennett
"For What It's Worth" (*Misfit Magazine*); "Déjà Vu" (*Out & About magazine poetry*)

Marion Brown
"Subway" (from the author's chapbook, *The Morning After Summer*); "Lament in Many Chapters for the End of the Earth and Love's Frailty" (*Kestrel*)

Jefferson Carter
"Nature Was My Church" (from the author's book, *Get Serious: New and Selected Poems*, Chax Press)

Alan Catlin
"From Bubbles to Bag Lady" (*Homestead Review*)

Joan Colby
"Squatter's Rights" (*Midwestern Gothic*)

Beth Copeland
"Keeping Time" (*Kakalak*)

James M. Croteau
"Cover Boys" (*Assaracus: A Journal of Gay Poetry*)

Laura Foley
"Ode to My Feet" (*Women's Voices for Change*)

Julie Fowler
"Removing the Homeless from Church" (Honorable Mention in the *The Bridge* 2010 Poetry Contest [Texas] and published in the 2011 anthology *From Under the Bridges of America*)

Karen Greenbaum-Maya
"Dignitas" (*Sow's Ear Poetry Review*); "Birdie" (*Off the Coast*)

Nancy Gustafson
"On the Edge" (*Lucidity Poetry Journal*); "Aunt Saphrana Counsels" (*My Kitchen Table,* Sweet Pea Press)

M. Ayodele Heath
"On Closing Woodruff Park, Atlanta (for renovation for the 1996 Summer Olympic Games)" (from the author's book, *Otherness,* Brick Road Poetry Press. Also published in *Eclectic Literary Forum; eyedrum periodically;* and *The Southern Poetry Anthology, Volume V: Georgia,* Texas Review Press)

Lynn Hoffman
"after the ocean left town" (*New Verse News* and *Valentrange*)
"River Song" (*Thunderclap*)

Janis Butler Holm
"Why He Won't Eat the Hot Meal So Charitably Provided" (*Red River Review*)

Karen Paul Holmes
"Flowers for You, Japan" (*Pirene's Fountain* anthology: *Sunrise from Blue Thunder*)

Paul Hostovsky
"Pearl in Bubble Wrap" (from the author's book, *A Little in Love a Lot,* Main Street Rag); "Rewind" (from the author's book, *The Bad Guys,* FutureCycle Press)

Joseph Hutchison
"The Gulf" (earlier version in *Poets for Living Waters*)

Laura M. Kaminski
"Educating the Creek" (*RiverLit* in "100 Words" category)

Robert S. King
"The Light Sedative of Dark" (*Spoon River Poetry Review*); "Mirror at the Speed of Light" (*Neonbeam* [U.K.]); "Strategy for Longevity" (*Eunoia Review*)

Lidia Kosk, translated by Danuta E. Kosk-Kosicka
"The Clock's Ticking" (*niedosyt/reshapings,* Oficyna Literatów i Dziennikarzy POD WIATR, Poland)

Carolyn Kreiter-Foronda
"The Bay's Tributaries" (*The Clinch Mountain Review* and *River Country*); "Homeless on Independence Avenue" (from the author's book *Contrary Visions* by Carolyn Kreiter-Kurylo [now Kreiter-Foronda], Scripta Humanistica)

Judy Kronenfeld
"At the YW Indoor Spa" (*Adanna Literary Journal*); "Her Vacated House" (*Valparaiso Poetry Review*)

Lori Lamothe
"Museum of Natural History" (*Cream City Review*); "Cave of the Great Galleries" (*Seattle Review*); "American Primitive" (*Fogged Clarity*); "Gray Sisters to Perseus" (*Linebreak*); "Road Trip to Forever" (from the author's chapbook, *Diary in Irregular Ink,* ELJ Publications)

Laura LeHew
"Apis Mellifera" (*The Incongruous Quarterly*)

Cynthia Linville
"No Exit" (from the author's book, *Out of Reach,* Cold River Press)

Catherine McGuire
"Squatter's Flag" (*Green Fuse*)

Marjorie Maddox
"Between States" (*Fiddleblack*)

James B. Nicola
"The Sack Man and the Suitcase" and "Another vase of flowers" (from the author's book, *Manhattan Plaza,* WordTech Communications)

Lynn Pedersen
"How to Speak Nineteenth Century" (*New England Review*); "The Rift" (*Comstock Review*); "At Forty" (*Chattahoochee Review*); "My Grandmother Peels Apples for Sauce" (from the author's book, *Theories of Rain,* Main Street Rag); "How to Move Away" (*Cider Press Review*)

Connie Post
"Extremities" (*Pirene's Fountain*); "Your Doorstep" (*California Quarterly*)

Mary Ricketson
"Stones at Sunset," "Walnut," and "Alacrity" (from the author's book, *Hanging Dog Creek,* FutureCycle Press)

Linwood Rumney
"Low Tide in Penobscot Bay" (*Carolina Quarterly*)

Sarah Russell
"Urban Sovereign" (*Misfit Magazine*)

Eric Paul Shaffer
"Yadokari: Hermit Crab, Okinawa" (from author's book, *Portable Planet: Poems,* Leaping Dog Press)

Lucille Gang Shulklapper
"Aging" (*Bear Creek Haiku*); "Old Woman Plays Piano" (*Long Story Short*)

J. J. Steinfeld
"Until the Paperwork Is Done" (*Grey Borders* and reprinted in the author's book, *Misshapenness,* Ekstasis Editions)

Meryl Stratford
"Elegy with Backward Clocks" (*Blue Hole* and reprinted in the author's chapbook, *The Magician's Daughter,* YellowJacket Press)

Wally Swist
"Amputee, Miami, 1959" (*Winding Paths Worn through Grass,* Chicago, IL: Virtual Artists Collective, 2012); "In the Shade of a Cave" (*Invocation,* Beaumont, TX, Lamar University Press, 2015)

Laurence W. Thomas
"Aging" (from the author's book, *Songs Sacred and Profane,* Xlibris Corporation)

Sara Toruño-Conley
"Mother's Aftermath" (*Found: Fiction and Poetry,* Wordrunner eChapbooks)

Lillo Way
"11th and Pine" (*The Bear Deluxe*); "Celestial Fantasy for Dr. Alzheimer" (*Common Ground Review*); "High Winds" (*Yemassee*); "Foraging" (*Third Wednesday*)

Richard Widerkehr
"Homeless" (*The Way Home,* Plain View Press, Austen TX)

Diana Woodcock
"Dugong" (forthcoming in the author's book, *Under the Spell of a Persian Nightingale,* WordTech Communications); "Desert Ecology 19: Angiospermae—Dicotyledoneae" (forthcoming in *The Desert's Botanical Bounty: Poems from the Heart of the Arabian Desert*)

Cover artwork, "Hospital Nightmare," by Maxwell Hamilton; cover and interior book design by Diane Kistner; Gentium Book Basic text with Arial Black and ITC Anna titling

About FutureCycle Press

FutureCycle Press is dedicated to publishing lasting English-language poetry books, chapbooks, and anthologies in both print-on-demand and Kindle ebook formats. Founded in 2007 by long-time independent editor/publishers and partners Diane Kistner and Robert S. King, the press incorporated as a nonprofit in 2012. A number of our editors are distinguished poets and writers in their own right, and we have been actively involved in the small press movement going back to the early seventies.

The FutureCycle Poetry Book Prize and honorarium is awarded annually for the best full-length volume of poetry we publish in a calendar year. Introduced in 2013, our Good Works projects are anthologies devoted to issues of universal significance, with all proceeds donated to a related worthy cause. Our Selected Poems series highlights contemporary poets with a substantial body of work to their credit; with this series we strive to resurrect work that has had limited distribution and is now out of print.

We are dedicated to giving all of the authors we publish the care their work deserves, making our catalog of titles the most diverse and distinguished it can be, and paying forward any earnings to fund more great books.

We've learned a few things about independent publishing over the years. We've also evolved a unique, resilient publishing model that allows us to focus mainly on vetting and preserving for posterity the most books of exceptional quality without becoming overwhelmed with bookkeeping and mailing, fundraising activities, or taxing editorial and production "bubbles." To find out more about what we are doing, come see us at futurecycle.org.

www.ingramcontent.com/pod-product-compliance
Lightning Source LLC
Chambersburg PA
CBHW061603110426
42742CB00039B/2736